WHAT WOULD LOVE DO NOW?

RE-CREATING FAMILIES
GETTING BACK TO A PLACE OF LOVE AFTER DIVORCE

BY KAREN WINTER

FIRST EDITION

ISBN (0-9742246-1-8)

MISSION STATEMENT

My goal is to inspire people to create loving relationships and to help them realize their power of creation and choice. I hope to reawaken them to the undeniable truth that we are all deserving, magnificent beings. I encourage everyone to direct their powers and energy in the highest and most positive way possible, which is love.

WITH LOVE AND GRATITUDE...

I wish to thank my family for helping me always in all ways. Having their love and support has been essential in becoming the me, that I am. Thank you, mom, dad, Kelly, Jav, Ingrid, Terry, David and most of all my two incredible children, Niky and Brontë, who bring unconditional love and playfulness into my life everyday.

I want to thank my friends and family who came to my very first workshop with open minds and hearts and allowed me to introduce this work in its roughest form.

Thank you to my friends who have remained loving and supportive through very challenging times, and who have helped me stay on my path.

Thank you to all the incredible women I have been blessed to know and work with at Cedros Soles. You have loved me and accepted me as I am and encouraged my work.

Thank you to Roy and Jennifer Moranz who developed my website and helped format this book. They have great creative ideas and enormous patience with my lack of computer skills!

Finally, I thank Sheila Kramer who edited this book and read it no less than thirty times. I will remember with fondness all the nights working together punctuated by visits from her beloved cat Arnie. Sheila has patience, humor and a wonderful talent with commas!

CONTENTS

CHAPTER 1: ANOTHER WAY 7
This is not the only way just another way

CHAPTER 2: MY STORY 11
This is where I came from, but not who I am

CHAPTER 3: SETTING INTENTIONS 24
Who do you want to be and what do you want to create?
A guide for creating your life

**CHAPTER 4: LETTING GO OF THE OLD VISION OF YOUR
FAMILY** 29
Going through grieving and loss
Letting go of the past and starting the future

CHAPTER 5: ACCEPTING THE GIFTS 38
Taking responsibility for your part of a relationship
Looking at the deeper meaning of a relationship
Gaining new knowledge of yourself

CHAPTER 6: GETTING BACK TO A PLACE OF LOVE 48
Defining and practicing forgiveness
Viewing yourself and your partner through new eyes
Looking anew at intentions

CHAPTER 7: CREATING CHANGE NEEDS SUPPORT 59
The power of changing a thought
Asking for help from friends and family
Commitment to positive energy and to a positive self

CHAPTER 8: LETTING YOUR CHILDREN KNOW 70
Telling your children the truth
Sharing your love story with your children
Letting your kids know where they came from

CHAPTER 9: HONORING YOUR CHILDREN'S FEELINGS AND YOUR OWN *77*

      Validating emotions and using reflective listening skills

      Avoid owning your children's feelings

      Allow your children their experience

CHAPTER 10: NEW LABELS AND NEW PARTNERS *86*

      The power of positive language

      New mantras to add positive power

      Accepting new members into your family

CHAPTER 11: REDISCOVERING YOURSELF *97*

      Taking care of yourself

      Deciding who you are and what you want from life

      Learning to love yourself

CHAPTER 12: THE PROCESS *109*

      It is not about the destination, but the journey

      It is all cyclical, and we are constantly creating together

CHAPTER 1

ANOTHER WAY

If you have begun to read this and it speaks to you, there is a reason. The reason is that you are ready to hear the message of these pages. You are ready for a change in yourself that will impact your whole family. This book is about re-creating families in a way that works for you. This is my way, but it is not the only way. I began to re-create my family five years ago and it is still a work in progress. I was frequently asked how my family had the relationship that it does. In particular, people were most often astonished by the incredible relationship I have with my former husband. People recommended others speak with me because I had what they called the "dream divorce" or the "perfect divorce". This always made me smile inside because I came to realize that I did, indeed, have the perfect divorce. It led me to where I am now and sent me on a journey inward to heal.

The reality is that my divorce was probably no different from many marriages that end. It was full of loss, anger, hurt, sadness and fear. I was compelled to finally leave my marriage upon realizing that I was so filled with these emotions that I knew it was time to leave or soon I would not be well physically either. Toward the end of my marriage I no longer recognized myself when I looked in the mirror--- where had I gone? I was much too thin and no longer taking healthy care of myself. I had become compulsive in my behaviors, trying desperately to regain control of a life that was completely out of control.

My current relationship with my children's father functions like a marriage relationship. Time, consideration and communication are required, because we are still a family. This key realization hit me from the very start and led me to create a vision of what I wanted my family to be. Making this vision a reality required diligent work. There are communication needs, considerations for the children and, still, a need to be good to one another.

Coming back from a retreat last New Year, I envisioned writing about my family and what had brought us to where we are now. When I sat down to write in the journal my sister had given me for the retreat, I quickly jotted down ten chapter headings. I put the notebook away for a period of nine months and during that time went through a lot of changes. Then something happened which led me to pull it back out and start this whole process. Suddenly, I was willing to let go of fear and doubt. I actually became aware of this fear and doubt in my life long before, but I was not ready to part with it. I took charge of my life and no longer let fear, my lifelong companion, control me. The words in the following pages are what I believe in passionately and wholeheartedly. I believe in possibilities, I believe in the human spirit and I believe in the mastery of love. The combination of all three is very powerful. I now understand that we are all very powerful and responsible for the use of our power everyday, in every decision, and in every interaction.

I realize that I could never be where I am today without all of my life experiences. I am also aware that every decision I have ever made has led me to where I find myself right now. I found that for much of my life I separated myself from the whole. I separated myself from my own love and, therefore, Divine love. This can be a very isolating and painful existence. Until I considered my alternatives, I was very willing to live this way. I went on creating in my life in a manner that was unmindful or unconscious. It was at the end of my marriage that I realized how I had been creating and this made me very unhappy and unfulfilled. This moment led me to a series of discoveries about myself that helped me to understand *me* and how *I* operated.

I read a series of books that were helpful; which I later list. I also began to develop new habits, which helped me to create in a new way. I started becoming more conscious of my choices and my own power of creation in my life. I also became more aware of my thought patterns and, therefore, was able to work on changing them. They were quite negative in content and I started to develop new positive thought patterns. This greatly affected my life and remains an ongoing process that I have not yet mastered. I am writing about things that I have discovered which help me tremendously and which I still practice daily in my life. Practice helps us to master skills. This is the practice in life.

I wanted to re-create my family in a way that felt good, safe and loving. We all want to be loved, to be valued and to belong. We might divert our attention to money and possessions, however, we soon find out that these things are not fulfilling in any deep soulful way in our lives. We find voids and holes, which we strive to fill. Yet underneath, it is all about love or the lack of it that we have in our lives. Most often, the lack comes from ourselves and not from others. How we interact with others is just a reflection of how we see ourselves. It took me a very long time to fully understand this idea. It took me much longer to get to a place to celebrate and to love myself. Often in our relationships, we are the first ones to abandon ourselves, but we feel it is our partners who have done the abandoning.

We are still families after divorce or separation, and we can create whatever we want. It takes time as well as intention. Your partner might not initially understand what it is you are trying to achieve. My parenting partner asked me outright, "What do you want? I just don't get it!" I then told him about my hopes and dreams regarding our family and our future. It still took time to understand fully and then to "join in" as he put it, but we are definitely working our way there. It has been five years now, and he says he does not know if we would have created this if I had not led us here. He wants to participate in this creation and as does his wife. I believe the reason is that it feels good to belong and to be loved. We can transform our families into this kind of safe haven if we so choose.

This is the opportunity to see ourselves, and our partners anew. We will be together for the rest of our lives. We have children together and will be grandparents together. We can make this bond into anything we like. Which do you choose---fiery foes or peaceful, loving co-parents who support one another? One book on divorce labeled couples according to their modes of communication. At the time, my husband and I were fiery foes and I felt so locked into this label. I felt hopeless, as though we would stay there forever because we had so much anger and hurt to work through. I realized that we can always work through any issues we face; we are never stuck unless we choose to be. We can all get back to a peaceful place even if it is not possible to be together. This requires forgiveness and release. It is possible to release our partners from our lives peacefully. There is a lot of material written about forgiveness and release work. We can continue to re-create in many ways and adjust and grow together just like any family does, but it takes intention and making the choice to do so.

The following chapters outline how my journey back to believing in and loving myself helped me to re-create my family after divorce. It all started by creating a vision of what I wanted and who I wanted to be. I write this not as a prescription of the way to get to a good place, but as a springboard from which to develop new ideas and ways to create. When we open ourselves up to life's possibilities, the limits we so long ago placed upon ourselves no longer confine us. This is about endless possibilities. We are powerful creators. As our thoughts create our reality and we are in control of our thoughts, we can, in essence, create anything we want. I encourage you to create in any way that feels good to you within your family. I find that I am creating everyday within my family. We are all constantly changing. Thus, our families move and grow accordingly. As families living in one house must adapt to constant change, so too must families adjust living in two homes. This process demands communication and attention, as does any relationship. Focusing these efforts helps us get back to a place of love.

CHAPTER 2

MY STORY

This is my story, but *I am* not my story. Instead, I am a creation of my own making. My background, however, helped me to create exactly what I came here to experience and to learn. I still have tendencies stemming from my background, but my life experience has taught me to let go of old practices that no longer work for me and to adopt new ones that do. This is always an ongoing process. After my divorce, I began my healing by looking at who I was and how I created my life.

I grew up primarily with my mother, my sister and my brother. My parents divorced when I was five, and my father chose to be a weekend dad with visits twice a month. Their separation was very traumatic. My mom and dad found themselves unable to be in the same room together for quite a few years after they were apart. Even when they were able to be together some ten years later, my parents never really let go of the hurt and anger they carried from their relationship.

My father did not allow emotional closeness between himself and others. I consistently found myself trying to excel at something to get his attention and approval (love). He was an athlete, a successful businessman and quite intelligent; despite all that, he was an alcoholic. My father was never abusive emotionally or physically, but he was unavailable. He did the best he could with the tools he was given from his family. My dad had a lot of problems that he was unwilling to sort out and release. This affected me as a child and I felt unworthy of his attention or praise. I took his actions and his way of life personally and made it about me. My father, I believe, felt that girls needed a lot less investment of time and emotion because they would most likely just end up raising children. In contrast, he believed boys needed much more guidance because they would do more in their lives. I think this was the idea he was given in his family growing up, as well.

Toward the end of his life, my father and I spent two weeks together at my home. I was pregnant with my first child and he was recuperating from surgery. He was completely sober (without alcohol) for the first time that I could remember. We spent our days together talking about life, and I shared with him all my childhood emotions. I told my father how I doubted my worth in relation to his show of love for me. I explained how my uncertainty regarding his love led me to endeavor many things in order to gain his praise. I also expressed to him how happy I was about the things I had done because of the gifts they brought me. My dad, in turn, shared his feelings of love for me and my siblings---stating his love was always there without question. My dad also expressed his love for my mother and revealed his biggest regret was that their marriage ended. It was amazing and powerful to realize that love was all there ever was. Somehow we complicated our communication, turned it around and imagined that there was not love, or at least not enough. This was a powerful time between us. My dad died five years later due to complications from his alcoholism and lifestyle. Ironically, it was my mother, my sister and I who were there in the last moments of his life. I will always remember my father's struggle to speak to us as he knew he was dying. After we each said goodbye and that we loved him, he still seemed anxious. We finally told my dad we knew he loved us, and he became peaceful. I will always believe in his love.

My mother struggled to raise three children on her own. She clearly had self-worth issues that went unresolved and unaided. During my early years, she was emotionally unavailable due to her self-doubt. She had been brought up in an environment that did not celebrate who she was as a young woman. She was not given many tools as a young woman raising children. She was however, there with love and care and she made sure our needs were taken care of always. It is difficult to capture the essence of my mother then and now because there is so much to her. In some ways, we grew up together in that we were on a journey to discover and develop self-love. There are some similarities in the way we created our lives and how we saw our relationships with our mates. I always sensed, a certain fragility in my mother that led me to

12

want to take care of her and shoulder more responsibility at home. This would mark how I created relationships for a long time to come.

My mother and I went through some difficult times together. We faced them again when I started therapy two years after I was married. We spoke about things in the past and started a healing and forgiving process. Over the last six years, my mother and I have each learned to hold ourselves and one another, with compassion for the people we were then and to love the people we are now. It has been quite a journey.

My earliest memories are of fear and loneliness. I am convinced much stems from my parents struggle with who they were and what they had created together--- leaving little energy to devote to children. I remember always being fearful as a child. This was not because I was harmed, but due to the precarious circumstances into which I was born. Later on, I associated the fear with what others might think of me, or my own lack of worth. I felt profound loneliness, because no one was emotionally available when I was young. I know now, as an adult, why my parents were so unavailable. I can understand their utter preoccupation with their fear, hurt and unhappiness. They were searching for themselves.

When my brother, the eldest sibling, turned thirteen he moved in with my dad. I lived with my mother and sister, and we communicated in a very feminine oriented style. My mom had utter faith in my sister and me to make our own decisions throughout most of our teen years. As a result, we were quite conservative compared to most of our friends. We never wanted to cause our mom any problems. We had already started on a path of taking responsibility for others and trying to keep everyone happy. I worked hard at school and had a job on the weekends with my dad. Upon turning fifteen, I had a job after school and helped my mother as much as possible by being independent. When I was eighteen, I began my studies at the University of California in San Diego. I spent two years at UCSD, and then left for a summer program in Paris. Instead of a month, I stayed for a year. I was an au pair and still have a wonderful connection with the family with whom I lived during that time. I came home and went back to work and school with a vengeance in order to finish my education and return to France.

I never made time for dating or romance, always keeping my focus on my studies. Two years later, my sister said she wanted to introduce me to her friend, Javier. She felt his international background would interest me. I remember clearly the night we met. My sister arranged it all. She brought a friend of hers and Jav brought a friend of his. I arrived late after work. Later, I was told that Jav knew immediately who I was when I walked in the door, and informed my sister I had arrived. I remember thinking how happy and playful he seemed. I found both of these qualities very attractive because I did not embody either. There was such a lighthearted quality to him. I was always very serious, hard working and responsible. Along came this person who was everything I was not---joyful, playful, happy and confident that all was possible in life. The world was his playground. His exuberance was infectious. That night, Jav told his parents he had met the woman he would marry!

I was mesmerized by Jav, and he was by me. I began to believe that everything was possible and life could be wonderful. I also really believed in love with him-- the kind that never ends. We played, had fun and loved each other. We decided to get married within three months. I was twenty-three at the time and Jav was twenty-seven. We set a date for a year from then. We spent that year playing, traveling and enjoying each other. I went on my first trip with his family at Christmas time. I quickly realized that Jav was different with his family than when he was alone with me. He finally told me that he was always worried about what they thought of him. This played out dramatically later in our marriage.

Looking back now, there were other signs that the relationship would be complicated with his family, but I did not pay attention to them. I ignored these portents because of my age, and I lacked the knowledge to interpret them. If I saw the same signs now, I would be able to interpret them more easily. I believe that everything happens for a reason. I had to create this relationship just as it was in order to become me as I am now.

Jav and I were inseparable during our courtship. I remember people used to say that we were in our own little world. They were right. I felt so utterly loved by this man. Jav's love felt wonderful and unlike anything I had ever experienced. I felt like a starving person at a banquet. I was absolutely unquestioning in his love for me and in mine for him. Jav and I would spend hours daydreaming about where we would live and how we would live our lives. We would dream about our children constantly and then practice making them. We spent a lot of that year planning our wedding, but we did not live together. Jav lived with his parents, and I resided with a roommate while I went to school. We decided we wanted living together to be a brand new experience.

Our wedding was beautiful. It was June, and the Spanish-style church was warm and intimate. My dress was made of the luscious Thai silk Jav's mom had brought back from her travels. I felt like a fairy princess marrying her prince. Jav and I were so moved by the moment and our own depth of emotion that we cried all through our vows. After the ceremony, we had a wonderful reception at a local hotel and celebrated with our family and friends. The next day, we left for a three-week honeymoon.

I realized on our trip that my husband's ties to his family were very strong, so much so that he called them frequently from wherever we were. It became obvious that our families and their ways were very different from one another. Our differences became markedly divisive throughout the next eight years of our life together.

When Jav and I returned from our honeymoon, issues began to immediately arise with my husband's family. There were constant misunderstandings and a lot of big emotions. I took all of this personally, and Jav was caught in the middle. He was very clear on how to handle the situation because he grew up in the system, but I was a newcomer and did not understand. Nonetheless, I often found myself taking responsibility for what had happened between us by making it my fault. This would lead me to try harder to please his parents and to win their love. When I tried to speak to my husband, he was unwilling to hear me. Lending credence to my thoughts would require Jav to change a lifetime of learned behaviors and beliefs about his family. I realized I could not make my husband see his family differently, because he was not ready. I took Jav's unwillingness to listen to me as a sign that perhaps his love for me had diminished. Later, when he would not believe that my hurt was genuine, I again took this to mean a lessening of love between us. I took everything personally.

Our financial situation was becoming tenuous, the extent of which I was unaware. The large sums of money with which Jav dealt always intimidated me. I assumed he knew how to manage extensive amounts of money, because he came from this kind of background. He was very conservative with money when we first married, and I felt reassured by that. When we started to face financial problems, he became quite risky in his investment decisions, which in turn diminished my feelings of security. My husband owned a successful import-export business and was doing well when we married, but the political cabinet changed and his contacts disappeared. Jav then became involved in capital investment, risking our savings in a series of very bad investments. I implored Jav to stop misusing our savings in this manner, but he continued to lose our money and informed me only after steep losses. This caused more problems with the trust between us. As these issues grew so, too, did the emotional distance between us.

Four years after we were married, we were expecting our first born son, Nikolas. I found myself completely absorbed in the raising of our child at the expense of my relationship with my husband. It seemed easier to focus on my baby than to concentrate on what needed to be dealt with in my marriage. I was already having strong feelings about my marriage not working, yet I kept pushing them down and disregarding the messages. It seemed easier to deny my truth until it was no longer a matter of choice. The mounting problems with his family were punctuated by moments of calm. The grandchild gave us all a new focus. On the other hand, it put additional financial pressure on my husband.

Jav had not had a job with an income in three years at this point. We had purchased a piece of property and we were building a house. I realized later that my husband never had much training in responsibility growing up and this was all new territory to him. The pressure for Jav was enormous, I had the expectation that he was fully capable of providing for our family; Jav, however, lacked the necessary skills. My husband found himself solely financially responsible for a wife and a child. Jav continued with risky business deals and proceeded to lose our savings, always convinced that a big windfall of money was just around the corner. Two years later, we had our daughter, Brontë.

Jav decided to become a restaurateur and opened his own brewery/discotheque in a hip exclusive location downtown. His parents put money into the project. He had no experience in this field and had only a shoestring budget. Jav worked long hours all day and into the night. I argued against the restaurant because it seemed one more wild idea. Jav felt he was finally concentrating in one area as he thought I wanted him to do. This only served as a point of contention between us as we were never together and had nothing to say when we were. Our emotional and physical relationship was almost nonexistent. I had isolated myself from him in almost every way. I felt abandoned with two children and sensed financial disaster looming ahead. Jav felt abandoned and unsupported by me and unsuccessful in his endeavors as a businessman. We were clearly at odds.

We started having problems with our checking account. I found my husband had applied for a loan to put more money into the restaurant, using our house as collateral without discussing it first. This was the last straw for me. I knew I could not live with his wild, reckless financial nature. Nor could I trust that what he said was the truth. But I knew his intentions were always good. Jav never intended to cause financial instability, but his ways of providing stability never worked. Instead of revising his plan, he repeatedly continued along the same path.

I will never forget the horrible moment in the stairwell of our home when I said I needed to separate, because I could not live like this anymore. It was something that my soul was demanding for a long time, but I could not give voice to the emotions and demands. Finally, I was stating my truth, but my truth felt like I was destroying another that I loved. Even though we were living with such anger and resentment between us, I loved him and did not want to hurt him. But I could not stay any longer or I knew I would not be well. I had become horribly thin, compulsive in my behaviors, and unable to maintain our public façade in light of our undeniable private truth.

This started a six-month period of turmoil. I discovered that our savings had been completely emptied. Our children's college funds were gone. There was nothing. Earlier, Jav was too afraid to tell me the truth, so he doctored investment papers to show me we were safe and secure. He moved out, and I sent my children to my mother's while I opened the doors to my home to sell all our belongings. I earned enough to live frugally for six to eight months. I sold our home, and Jav reclaimed the profit as right of reimbursement from his parents' financial gifts in the past. He held the money for five months. We settled the children's living arrangements and visitation, but agreeing on finances took a long time. Finding my equilibrium was emotionally difficult and draining. I am sure Jav felt similarly. We both felt left adrift and quite afraid. He demanded that I put any funds I received in the children's name and claim nothing for myself. There was always a sense of mistrust financially in his family that permeated everything, as though people were only after them for their money. I declined the conditions Jav placed on the money, but did promise to use the funds in raising our children. He agreed after six months and signed our agreement. We were now divorced.

The year ahead of us would be one of rebuilding and a lot of hard work. Here we are six years later with much to show for it. The following pages outline how we arrived to where we are now, but by no means indicate that we are done. There is always more to learn and new experiences to share. We are always recreating and changing, causing ripples or sometimes waves. We all need to be strong calm swimmers and focus on our direction.

Our Wedding Photo

On our honeymoon in Australia, July 1988

Our son Nikolos, age 18 months

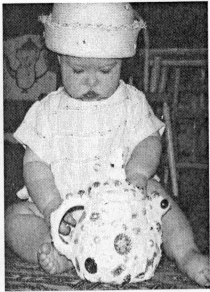

Our daughter Brontë, her first birthday

Christmas 1995, our last together

Celebrating Brontë's ballet recital altogether, 1998

The first photo of all of us together, Christmas 1998

Ingrid, Niky, Brontë and I in the jumper – Celebrating Brontës 6th Birthday

Jav, Niky, Brontë and I on our ski trip, 2000

CHAPTER 3

SETTING INTENTIONS

The most important step to begin this process of re-creation is setting an intention toward which to work. Determining your objective enables you to focus on the choices. This is so important because, it helps in the choices you make about who you are and how you treat yourself and others in your life. The title of this book, What Would Love Do Now?, is my guiding question in creating my intentions. When I am uncertain as to how to handle a situation or a conflict I ask myself, "What would love do now?" This helps me to be centered and act in a manner that is respectful and caring to all involved. Once you create a vision for your family—whether that vision requires teamwork, open communication, trust, development of new skills, etc.--- you can choose who you want to be within that model.

Deciding who you want to be demands recognizing who you really are. You must remember who you are and get in touch with the wonder of your being. I believe we all come here with a soul purpose and incredible gifts to share. However, we often forget our beauty and we do not give ourselves love, compassion or gentleness. We might even share these qualities with others, but not with ourselves. We lack training in celebrating the self. We rarely discuss this in our culture. Our parents were not brought up this way nor were their parents; this is not an issue of blame but an issue of change. We must all participate in self-celebration in order to create in a new way and help our children grow in this spirit or, rather, with Divine Spirit.

Children inherently know how to embrace this idea of self-love. They are sure of themselves, but are often taught another way, which makes them less self-assured. Therefore, we must get back to a place of self-love, get in touch with our true beings and avoid imparting negativity. This can be aided by meditation, yoga, a spiritual practice and related books. This process of re-creation requires the faith that we are all inherently wonderful and loving beings and are all created in the likeness of Spirit. We all come from the same place, the same energy, and the same being--God. What would it be like if we all remembered who and how divine we are? How would our actions be toward each other? The doubt demons would diminish or disappear completely. By this I mean that there would always be the assumption that everyone is doing his/her best. This helps lead to acceptance and compassion rather than to judgment and anger. Competition and the need to feel superior would no longer exist.

My vision was a creation to comfort myself at the time of my separation. I envisioned my husband and myself as friends, talking to one another and sharing our lives. I saw us being a team - raising our children, supporting them during their lives, sharing birthdays and holidays altogether. I found this comforting because I felt such a sense of loss over our separation (even though I asked for it). I felt scared and alone because I was losing someone I loved. I was also hurt and angry. My vision gave me the comfort and strength to believe that Jav and I could find our way back to love after all that we had shared and created together. What I now realize is that this time enabled me to see a role for myself in the future. If I wanted to get back to love, I had to start first by loving me. Somewhere along the line, I had fallen out of love with me.

A woman in my workshop shared that merely setting an intention to let go of her anger toward her husband helped her tremendously. She felt as though she were somehow carrying less weight. She had not even begun the work or the process, yet found it enormously comforting to have set a direction for herself that was toward the light. Setting the intention is a very powerful step, because it is the first move toward change and a new creation.

I believed in love. Recognizing this, I set an intention to create a supportive and loving foundation for myself and my family. This helped to strengthen my faith that love existed even in moments of complete despair. During our separation, I struggled to reconcile my vision of who I wanted to be with the hurt, angry person that I was. I constantly negotiated internally to decide how I wanted to act in this situation. Divorce can be extremely difficult because it brings to the surface our common fears about not being loved. We often cite money or another person for ending our relationship, but it all traces back to not feeling loved by another. I remember that when Jav and I discussed finances, our communication became very heated. I was afraid because I was a stay-at-home mom for four years and, suddenly, I was responsible for raising two children and paying the bills. My husband was angry and felt that he was being asked only for money. I realized, during this time, that I did not want to fight over money. In a sense, I would be reducing (the sum total of) our life together down to a dollar figure and lessening that which we had shared. I also knew that if we kept fighting over money, we would never come back to recognizing each other-- who we really were and had been for nine years together.

During our separation, my vision kept me centered. I waived my right to alimony, accepted (what my husband deemed) reasonable child support, and split with Jav the proceeds from the sale of our home. This was accomplished primarily through mediation rather than through attorneys. I say this not as a victim or an example of what another "should" do, but in order to share what worked for me. By sharing my experience, I hope to help others explore what would best work for them. I try to omit the word "should" from my vocabulary, because it connotes not doing the "right" thing. Only you know if what you are doing is really working for you by how it resonates with your being. When fear sets in about what others might think, I am reminded of a saying that is significant to me: "It's none of my business what others think of me." I learned this phrase from Terry Cole Whittaker, the acclaimed author/speaker. She used this quote as the title of her popular book. I suggest employing this quote when confronted by fear of judgment. Doing so helps you to focus on your vision and follow your path.

A year later, Jav and I began raising our children as a team (both emotionally and financially). We fostered a mode of communication that we both found helpful and healing. One of the most important lessons we learned, however, was how to put down our weapons and to stop re-acting to one another in the same old way. Each year I can plot the progress of our relationship, and I know that both of us feel more assured of ourselves and of what we have created together.

Jav and I now better understand who we were in the past and what we created during our marriage. We have both learned to see ourselves and one another, more compassionately and have, therefore, received the gifts of our relationship. There is nothing but gifts, because each relationship teaches us so much about ourselves-- who we are and what things make us react, both positively and negatively. It is not so much about the other person and who they are but rather, it is about who we are in relation to that other person.

Your life is a work of art in progress, everyday you begin with a blank canvas. Choose your palette, choose your brushes and begin to paint. This is your journey of self-discovery.

Create your vision. Visualize it coming true, add to it with details. Write about it and read it afterward. Watch as it becomes your reality. You have the strength within you to make this happen. Know that who you are and what you do make a difference in the world. Every action elicits a reaction. Your thoughts manifest your reality. As you turn your light on, you allow those around you to do the same.

SETTING INTENTIONS EXERCISE

1. What is your vision of your family?

    _____

    _____

    _____

    _____

2. Who do you want to be in that family? What is your vision of youself?

    _____

    _____

    _____

3. What can help you to realize your vision of yourself? What guiding question could keep you centered and remain within your vision?

    _____

    _____

    _____

    _____

    _____

4. What would help you keep on track? How can you implement this?

    _____

    _____

    _____

    _____

CHAPTER 4

LETTING GO OF THE OLD VISION
OF YOUR FAMILY

When I separated from Javier, I realized I had an array of emotions with which to deal. Loss was one of the many feelings I had; I truly felt I was losing a part of my family and my friend. I had to let go of the dream I held of what my family would look like. Even before I had my children, I held a vision or dream of what my life would be. I thought we would have three children with lots of lively interaction between us. I pictured my husband and myself as great parenting partners, involved with our children's lives as well as having time for our own relationship. I realize my dreams were not terribly different from those of others. When Jav and I separated, I had to let go of this dream and it felt like grieving after a death. I remember feeling so sad at times, being without a partner in life. There were so many occasions when I did not feel like we were a family, simply because there was not a father present. I had to constantly remind myself that we were still a family--we just looked different than before.

There were many moments of feeling sorry for myself, which were frequently followed by negative self-talk. It was a long time before I could (really) be gentle with myself and not judge my feelings. Sometimes, loneliness would allow my mind to imagine the possibility of reuniting with Jav and once again being a "family." And yet, I knew in my heart, I could not do this. I could not go back to the way I lived before. My unhappy feelings were enough to create doubts about whether or not I had made the "right" decision in separating. I used to struggle with the "rightness" or "wrongness" of my decision for my children although, I knew that I could not be happy within the marriage we had created. I also knew that staying together for my children was not the answer for me. I wanted to be able to show my children a happy and fulfilled mother, and I could not do that while married to my husband. When I reviewed the reasons for my decisions, I felt strengthened in my resolve to move forward.

One woman shared that in order for her to start this process, she had to acknowledge the grief she felt within herself over the fact that her marriage had ended. She realized it would be a process of grieving and that she needed to respect it and give it time. Part of her grieving process was to read old cards and letters from her husband, shed some tears and let them go. She also had to acknowledge that her life was not going to go according to the plan she had devised so long ago. She felt she needed to feel the sadness fully before she could allow herself the creative energy required to re-create her life with her children.

I remember having fears about parenting on my own. Could I manage the responsibility of making decisions alone? I had already been doing this in my marriage and yet it felt different now. I struggled with developing the self-confidence to handle all of my commitments. There was a feeling of being overwhelmed during the day or late at night, because there was no one to share the responsibility of raising the children. My parenting skills needed to grow along with my children's ages and needs. Learning new tools for handling their emotions was an enormous help.

I had fears of managing finances on my own. When I was married I did not like the way Jav controlled our finances, because his style was too risky for me. While I felt calmed that I was now in charge and knew what would be coming, I still, had to face the fear of the responsibility of being in charge. Could I do a good job managing the money on my own? I made some decisions about how to invest my savings. Of course, along the way there were some expensive lessons to be learned. I again trusted someone implicitly because they handled large sums of money all the time just as I had done with my husband. I realized that everyone's ideas about and ways of dealing with money are different. My goal was to stay at home until my children were in school before seeking outside employment. Until such a time, I had a small business in my home. My first investment advisor put me right into a high-risk fund, which he told me was the only way not to deplete my account. I lost an enormous sum of money on a turn in the market, but I learned a lot about the differences in language and being understood. My advisor was adamant he had conveyed the risk factor involved, and I felt as though I was clearly relaying (to him) my utter dependence upon this money for the next few years. We had obviously not understood each other's messages.

At one point, I convinced myself that my children would prefer being with their father, because he had a girlfriend. Their image conformed more closely to my mental picture of a family. When I look back now, I cannot believe all the tortures to which I subjected myself. There were, of course, moments when my children wanted to be with their dad---just as there were moments they wanted to be with me. I now realize this happens whether or not parents are married. When a child states he/she wants his other parent, we take this personally and feel we are lacking in some way. This is not the case; our children are simply stating what they need. This situation is more difficult to deal with when parents are divorced, because we can be out of balance until we are healed within our own hearts. Our children's choice is not a judgment against us unless we make it one.

One of my goals was to let go of anger. I was angry with my husband for our financial situation. I took a long time to realize that my anger toward Jav's family was due to my hurt feelings. It took me even longer to understand fully why I took everything as an indication of my unworthiness. I felt hurt because Jav did not believe me when I told him of his family's actions toward me. I took all of their actions toward me personally. I could not let anyone's behavior be their own without somehow including myself as being responsible. I felt hurt when Jav then recognized the problem and told me it was my fault for inciting his parents' anger. I felt hopeless when the problems continued. The hurt became layered over with anger, because the core issue had never been resolved. Healing entailed peeling back the layers and getting in touch with the hurt.

When I became aware of the hurt, I asked Jav to meet with me. We spent a couple of hours talking about our relationship. Jav was surprised to hear that I did not feel loved in our relationship, because he *did* love me. I then realized that he loved to the best of his ability for who he was then. I interpreted his love through my own filters at that time. Jav was not ready to confront who his parents were as people during our marriage, much less set personal boundaries for himself in relationship to them. Nor was he able to confront his own fears or problems with having a job and the responsibility of a family to support. But Jav did love. And so did I. We asked things of each other that we were not ready to do.

The key part of this healing was realizing that my husband always had good intentions. When I could see where Jav and I came from with compassion instead of judgment, my anger dissipated and I began to heal. At this point, I realized that I had a lot of attachment to the form that love took. In order to feel loved, love would or "should" have a certain composition. I was attached to form, which led to expectations. It is very difficult not to be disappointed in life when you have a set of expectations already in place. I had expectations of love—how it would look and how it would act. This led me down a long path of disappointment and false assumptions. I assumed that our love was lacking if my husband did not act in a certain way. Most often, Jav did not have any knowledge of my rules for love.

One exercise that helped me release anger was to step outside myself, relinquish my own view, and step into my husband's shoes. I really tried to see it from his perspective. Jav fell in love and got married. He tried to the best of his ability to have a job. He faced enormous challenges with his family and his wife in that they never got along. Regardless of the "side" with whom he spoke, he was always caught in the middle. Often, that caused him problems with both sides. His wife was pressuring him to look at his parents as people for the first time in his life. This was in direct opposition to how he had been raised. Jav was uncomfortable with his wife's views, and uncertain how to manage the situation. He just wanted to make his wife happy, but it never seemed clear how to do this. He felt frustrated and unappreciated. There was an emotional gulf growing between him and his wife, and he felt powerless to stop it. His wife stepped back from their physical and emotional relationship, which felt like rejection to him. He was

32

facing an enormous financial crisis and hiding it from his wife. He was dealing with his own fears, hurt and anger.

This exercise of examining Jav's behavior is not for the purpose of judging him "right" or "wrong". The goal is to understand how the other person feels from *his/her* perspective. The objective is to get from anger to compassion. I began to feel more compassion for Jav; I understood why he made the choices he did based on his background. Again, this is not blaming parents, but rather believing that they do the best they can based on the tools *they* have. We also do the best we can with the tools *we* have. When we realize that the tools with which we create no longer serve us, we can begin to let go of old ways and thoughts and work on adopting new ones. I always try to remember a lesson from my uncle. He taught me:

> No mistakes have been made, none are being
> made and none can be made. This is because
> we are all whole, perfect and complete just as
> we are and just as we are not. Ever-evolving
> consciousness is always rising, because Spirit
> is never still or dormant.

I no longer held anger in my heart for my husband when I really took the time to look at him from a different perspective. This practice proved useful when we were going through our divorce proceedings. My new perspective helped me to understand that even if Jav was angrily attacking me with an attorney, inside he was feeling hurt and fearful about being alone. The person who acts out the most often needs the most love. I know Jav needed reassurance at these times. He still had his children. He was a part of something, but it felt completely changed. Jav and I felt as though we were dangling, unattached to anything. We were off-balance and heading into unknown territory. Most often, the unknown produces fear. We had enormous fears.

I realized after all of this that we had different love languages. What meant and felt like love to me was different for Jav. I needed to rely on my abilities to communicate to him what felt loving to me and what I really wanted. I also had to take responsibility for never having asked Jav to choose between me and his family. I feared that he would neither, hear me, or respond and I was afraid to ask for what I wanted, because I thought I was unworthy. We have a responsibility to ask for what we want and to listen to each other's needs, as well. Often, our love languages are different simply due to gender differences. Frequently, they vary because we grew up with dissimilar examples of what love is between couples and in relationships.

Somewhere under the anger is hurt, and beneath that is the feeling of being unloved. It is painful when we do not feel cherished or honored by someone else. Yet, if we are filled with our own love for ourselves and really have faith in who we are, engaging in the fears and doubts of being unloved becomes difficult. All that does exist between human beings is love. The rest is merely a habit of letting our minds take charge, rather than our hearts. We are immersed in judgment, rather than compassion. Often we are attached to a preconceived image of love and never actually enjoy loves inherent beauty. We convince ourselves, at some point, that love must have a certain feel, look or embodiment. Therefore, if love shows up in a different form than that which we expect, we do not accept or recognize it at all.

LETTING GO OF THE OLD VISION OF YOUR FAMILY EXERCISE

1. Have you let yourself grieve for the loss? (for example: loss of a partner, a dream, a friend, expectations) In what ways?

    _____

    _____

    _____

    _____

    _____

2. How has holding onto the old vision of your family affected your life?

    _____

    _____

    _____

    _____

    _____

3. Create a ritual ceremony for yourself to let go of your relationship (for example: lighting a candle and saying a prayer of gratitude for the relationship, making a ceremonial fire and burning old letters and cards, taking a meditative walk on the beach and releasing sadness and loss to the universe).

    _____

    _____

    _____

    _____

    _____

    _____

4. What fears arise from creating life without your spouse? Walk down the path of *what ifs*, what will happen if your worst fear is realized? The goal here is to take the power away from the fear.

_____

_____

_____

_____

_____

5. Are you feeling anger toward your partner for the way in which your marriage was created? What is the cause for your anger? Looking at the cause, is there underlying hurt over the circumstances between you?

_____

_____

_____

_____

_____

6. Practice living your marriage from your partner's perspective. What can you better understand about that person from their point of view? Do you notice a shift toward compassion?

_____

_____

_____

_____

_____

7. After having understood better your partner's view-point, what do you think was his/her intention in your marriage at the beginning of your relationship? What was your intention at the beginning?

_____

_____

_____

_____

_____

8. How were your love languages different? Did the things that felt like love to you, feel that way to your partner and vice versa? What have you learned by looking at your own love language about how you accept or deny love in your life?

_____

_____

_____

_____

_____

_____

_____

_____

_____

_____

_____

_____

_____

_____

_____

CHAPTER 5

ACCEPTING THE GIFTS

The first step in accepting the gifts of a relationship is taking responsibility for its creation. We all co-create our relationships. We, just as our partners, are responsible for what we create. Sometimes, we engage in finger pointing and blame-games. Early on in my marriage, I appointed blame. I blamed my husband for not "protecting" me from his family's angry outbursts. I now know that I contributed to the nature of our relationship. I simply did not believe in my own ability to manage the situation with my in-laws. I also wanted my husband's support in dealing with them, but he was not ready to support me or deal with them. We instead chose blame and anger.

I had an inner fear that I was not worthy of love. This was a huge fear that became evident whenever I interacted with my in-laws. They mirrored my fear, and it became all consuming in my life. There is a widely held belief that we draw to us what we fear the most or what we most need to learn. These experiences show us there really is nothing to fear (because we made it up). I learned what fear stands for at a retreat I attended last year:

> **F**alse
> **E**vidence
> **A**ppearing
> **R**eal

I started to play the message to myself that I was unworthy and therefore, less. When I first met Jav's family, my self-doubts became magnified. They were quite wealthy, cultured, well-traveled and seemingly confident people. I thought that by joining such a family I could gain the confidence I lacked. We had a very difficult time communicating and accepting each other. I always took this personally. Their lack of love toward me proved that my fears of my unworthiness were valid. This was false, and yet, I was willing to believe it (F.E.A.R.). I learned after our divorce, that my in-laws were just as afraid as I. Under the pressure of the moment, however, I was not centered in order to be able to view them with compassion. I had very little compassion for myself back then. The lack of love and compassion I had for myself impacted all of my relationships.

Louise Hay, the internationally renowned healer, wrote in her book *The Power Within,* fear is about a lack of trust in ourselves. Because of that we do not trust life. We do not trust that we are being taken care of on a higher level, so we feel we must control everything on a physical level. Fear imposes limits on our minds and our ability to create fully in our lives as well. Releasing the fear in our lives opens up space for love and trust. Once we make this transition we will attract and create more of this in our lives.

God states, in Neale Donald Walsch's book 1 *Conversations With God And Uncommon Dialogues,*

> You have been taught to live in fear. You have been told about survival of the fittest and the victory of the strongest and the success of the cleverest. Precious little has been said about the glory of the most loving. When you choose the action love sponsors, then will you do more than survive, then will you do more than win, then will you do more than succeed. Then will you experience the full glory of Who You Really Are, and who you can be. The greatest teacher is the voice within you.

I now see that Jav and I mirrored each other emotionally. We had many fears and, together, we scared ourselves. Jav was not emotionally ready to leave his family and stand on his own. That gave his parents great power within our marriage. I was not ready to demand that I be treated with respect, and neither was Jav. We were alike and, therefore, attracted one another like magnets. Our universe works as a system of magnetic forces. We attract those who mirror who we are or who mirror our beliefs of ourselves. The presentation might be somewhat different, but there are similarities. Embracing these truths compelled me to reexamine the dynamics of my relationship with Jav and understand in what ways we were alike. Fear was the match - - fear of what others would think of us, fear that we would not be accepted and the underlying fear that we would not be loved. We all just want to love and to be loved. The amazing thing is that there was always love between my husband and me, and there still is. It has changed form since we first met, but while we were separating, both of us would have sworn that we were not loved by our partner.

There is a profound belief that you draw to you what you fear the most. I realized that from my childhood I had a fear of being without enough money. I remember there were some very lean times, when I was growing up with my mother. Yet we always had enough-- a place to live, food and clothes. But there were embarrassing moments when checks would bounce at the grocery store and we had to add everything up before getting to the check-out counter, because we now had to pay with cash. More than anything, I remember my mother's fear and embarrassment during those moments. As I grew older and was responsible for myself, I always had enough and put myself through college. Still, there was always this persistent fear underneath that one day there might not be enough. When I married my husband we had enough, and I had such a sense of security living with him. Jav seemed so capable and confident at the beginning. Then problems started to occur, and by the end of our marriage we found ourselves without enough and facing severe financial problems. We faced disaster and I manifested my worst fears. I also survived them and learned to depend on myself. I know I can always support my family. I remind myself of this daily.

I no longer fear that there will not be enough. My son, Niky, taught me a great lesson in this area. When he was old enough to read, he started reading people's signs in the street asking for help. Niky responded. He would ask me to stop and if he had his lunch box for that day he would offer whatever he had. Sometimes, he would ask me to go back home and pack something healthy for that person. I saw how much we had when we shared what we had with others. There was always enough to share.

When we forget who we are, it is easy to embrace the negative messages we often hear and turn them inward. The goal is to remember who we are and to realize we have embraced all the negatives about ourselves. We created a vision of ourselves and then manifested a life to go along with that vision. I no longer feel I am unworthy of love. I realize that no one else is either. We are all the same. We come from the same energy, the same Spirit, or whatever name feels comfortable be it God, Yahweh, Allah, or Spirit. We are all one. Remembering this has helped me to treat myself with more kindness and compassion (though I can still forget on occasion), and that is mirrored in the life I have now created. In essence, I created a life that helped me to remember who I am. I now know that my marriage was exactly what I needed to bring me back to me, even though it seemed painful at times. We create and invite others into our lives for reasons sometimes only known to us at a soul level. Trust and know that all is a gift. It takes living mindfully to accept the gifts. Sometimes the gifts are not revealed all at once, but over time.

A woman with whom I spoke was convinced that her husband was to blame for all that was wrong in her life. One day she realized that something in her had attracted him as her mate. She knew she needed to heal herself, that part of her that was open to his darkness, in order to change the course of her life. She started taking responsibility for creating a relationship with this person. This was the point at which she could take charge and create change for herself. She was empowered because she no longer felt like a victim.

I am not trying to tell the world to make peace with someone who is not well or who might be violent or dangerous. However, I am saying we must know why we are with these people. We can begin to heal that part of ourselves that is open to such an experience. These relationships are still gifts because they allow us the opportunity to look anew and to decide what we want to create now. We need to take the time to decide mindfully what it is we want to create. This requires changing our thoughts on the issues and conditions we wish to create.

There is always a deeper meaning to our relationships. When you look at past relationships, think about whom you were then as compared to now. What changes do you see? Our interaction with that other person has allowed us to experience ourselves. We see our responses, our reactions, and our ability to give and receive love. Relationships are always affected by whom we allow ourselves to be. Did we give ourselves permission to be our true selves? Did we believe in and love ourselves enough to share all our splendor with another? Or did we invite fear into our relationships and own every nuance of negativity as a possibility of our own unworthiness?

I know now, five years after my marriage has ended, that my husband loved me and on some level I knew it then. However, I felt unloved when Jav did not immediately believe me when I shared my hurt feelings over his parent's behavior. I asked for what I needed, and he was unable to give me that emotional support. Yet I never asked Jav to choose between his parents and myself because I was afraid. That was really about me. I took Jav's inability as a sign of my unworthiness. I was re-acting in the same (old) patterns I had been using all my life. My pattern was to take things personally and to make it about me. I did this until I realized that it no longer worked for me, because this reaction no longer reflected who I was. We do this often; we re-act in old ways until we realize it no longer works for us.

I continually doubted my father's love for me, because he did not show it in a way that I wanted. Yet, he did love me. I remember when I was in high school, I visited my dad for a weekend. He pulled a box from the top shelf of his closet and showed me his treasures he had kept for years. It was a shoe-box that held all of the cards and mementos my siblings and I had made for him in school over the years. I remember feeling surprised because my father did not seem very sentimental to me, yet here he was holding onto this collection of things we had made for him.

My relationship with my father was complicated because of the way I interpreted his actions. His actions were not always an indication of my worth as his daughter, yet I usually internalized things between us in a negative manner. It was important to my dad that his children go to college. Being a graduate himself, he saw enormous advantages to being formally educated. He promised all three of us that he would help us financially when it was time for us to attend. I was the only one to go to college and when it was my time to attend, my dad's attitude had changed. He said he would send me some book money and that was it. I felt stranded and frightened, I had always counted on my father's help, but it was now obvious it was not coming. I somehow, made my dad's decision not to help an indication that I was not worthy of his help. I did not consider that his disease (alcoholism) had progressed to such a level that he was not capable of making sound decisions anymore. In essence, he was another person during that time. Who he was, had nothing to do with me. I had a difficult time understanding this until much later in my life. In sum, I worked and put myself through college and the achievement was mine. None of this indicated that my father did not love me or find me worthy, but I appointed my own meaning to the situation and it was negative. I took it personally, again.

I drew my husband to me because I needed to experience what we created together. It helped me grow into the person that exists now. I am grateful for the creation, and my gratitude helped me to receive the gifts of my relationship with my husband. I have two incredible children from this marriage. I shared amazing love, joy, sadness, pain and sorrow with this man. This is what life is made of, and we certainly lived it fully and with passion. How could I turn my back on this person with whom I have shared so much life?

Having had this experience in my life, I realize I create differently now. I have changed as have my needs and desires. When we look again at our relationships and see clearly who we were; what made us act out or what exaggerated our fears, we can begin to heal that part of ourselves by being compassionate and gentle. We need to be as gentle as we would with our best friend when he/she shares their hurt. We need to nurture ourselves just as we would our children. In fact, we need to learn to nurture the child *within* us that still exists, but often gets pushed away or ignored.

I went to a hypnotherapist for a session based on caring for the child within. This involved getting in touch with the child I was during my childhood; who she was, how she felt, and if she felt loved and cherished. After identifying her needs, the goal was to take care of her. I reassured her that I loved her and would protect her and never abandon her. This ritual involved incorporating her into my being. The experience was soothing and comforting. Talk to your inner child and protect her/him, show her love and gentleness just like you would your own child. Honoring that part of you is a healing experience.

I am always amazed when I re-create my old patterns of behavior. When we ignore responsibility for our lives it is stunning how we re-live the same story again and again. Understanding does take consideration and time to look back at what we have created. How can we fully understand our relationship or ourselves unless we comprehend what we have created? This allows us more insight into who we are and heightens our ability to live mindfully instead of mindlessly. We can move forward when we look at who we have been and endeavor to know why. This leads to the question: What kind of relationship would you like to create in the future?

I invite people to look anew at their idea of forever. Many people I speak to use terms such as "failed marriage", "broken home", and "not being good at relationships". This is a collection of negative terms describing relationships that have ended. I think that relationships have not failed simply because they have ended or have changed. I learned a new concept from the acclaimed author/speaker, Neale Donald Walsch. He said, "Everything is meaningless until we give it meaning, and we can give things any meaning we want". I choose to give my relationship with my husband a positive meaning, because it gives me a positive outlook on my life. The fact that my marriage ended does not demean it in any way. The ending of our marriage was a catalyst for my husband and I to move forward and create a great friendship that is loving and caring. It feels good to us and is a good model for our children.

I knew a little girl who was trying to understand her mother's and father's love relationship. She said to her mother that their relationship was like a rose that had come to full bloom but had died. We never forget the beauty that a rose holds. This was incredibly poetic from a nine-year old. This metaphor always stayed with me throughout the years because it was so profound. The end of a relationship or a marriage does not mean that its beauty never existed or that it is rendered meaningless. It has merely changed form.

My uncle gave a blessing at my sister's wedding, and his message was very beautiful. He acknowledged the children of my sister's husband as proof that the love between he and his children's mother will never die. The love is alive in their children and always will be. We still have the ability to look at our lives and see beauty and meaning if we want, but it is a choice. It is our responsibility, how we create our thoughts and make our choices.

The presence of someone in our lives is a gift whether it lasts for a week, a month or years. The gift lies not in the time factor, but in the presence of love and the celebration of it. If love comes into your life, treasure it and live it fully even if it lasts only a short time. Love is still the most important thing that exists.

ACCEPTING THE GIFTS EXERCISE

1. Describe your marriage. What were the dynamics between you? What characterizes your relationship and your communication style?

_____

_____

_____

_____

_____

2. In what ways did you help to create this relationship?

_____

_____

_____

3. What attracted you to your partner?

_____

_____

_____

4. How did your partner fulfill you?

_____

_____

_____

_____

_____

5.   What were your needs going into this relationship?

_____

_____

_____

_____

6.   Did you and your partner mirror each other? In what ways?

_____

_____

_____

_____

7.   Did you allow yourself to share all of the parts of your character with your partner? Did you allow your partner to do this or did it create discomfort for you?

_____

_____

_____

_____

_____

    Set aside private time for the inner child work. Sit quietly and take some relaxation breaths. Visualize yourself as the child you were. Look into your eyes as you were a child. Notice the features of your young face. Ask your inner child what he/she wanted. Ask he/she if they felt loved. Listen to your child's answer. Now take this child into your arms and rock her/him. Make your solemn promise of love and care that you will devote to him/her. Let your child know how loved and important they are and that they will never be alone. Soothe this child as you would your own child. Gently picture absorbing this child into your being. Now take some deep rhythmic breaths and slowly come back to the awareness of the room.

CHAPTER 6

GETTING BACK TO A PLACE OF LOVE

Forgiveness was one of the first steps that enabled me to get back to a place of love. This is really a practice for the self more than for the other person involved. It is an act of selfishness. This idea can make people highly uncomfortable, because most of us have spent a lifetime being taught that selfish is a bad word. Basically, it means taking care of the self or considering the self. Amazingly, we are taught early on that selfishness is a negative and that we should think of others first. Yet, selflessness is really a practice for saints, and most of us came here for the human experience.

Forgiveness is an act for the self, in that it provides us with peace. As most of us have experienced recently, a life without peace is quite unsettling to say the least. We have choices and we can choose to remain unhappy, angry, bitter, hateful, sad, unfulfilled or we can choose happiness, gratitude, compassion, caring and love. Which emotions sound better for life partners? I choose the second set. To get there, however, I had to do the work involved. This does not mean that you can never feel negative emotions because they are normal human experiences. Staying locked in a negative emotional state is something else entirely. The key to moving through emotions is to let the emotion move through you. Let the emotion you are feeling come and just be with it. Do not judge it, just note it and feel it. By experiencing the emotion, you can then let it go.

Once I went through the stages of seeing Jav with new eyes, I was able to get to a place of forgiveness. I no longer blamed him for my unhappiness, because I was able to take responsibility for my part in what we had co-created. Events in our relationship were never one-sided. They seldom are, but are we ready to take responsibility for our relationships in this way? Taking responsibility for co-creating took my husband out of the villain seat and placed him beside me once again. Trying to understand

Jav's experience in our relationship helped me to get to a place of compassion for him.

This exercise also helped me to look again at the very people I had been so hurt by and angry with for nine years of my life (more when I consider I carried these feelings after our separation). Jav's parents were doing the best they could. Here again, they were not to blame for our relationship. We most likely scared each other and in that fear created a multitude of problems between us. I realized that I shared loving and tender moments with my in-laws. I now know that this is what made their angry moments so hurtful for me. I would then react with hurt and anger and worsen the situation. They grew up with distinctly different backgrounds than my own. Which, once again, accounted for completely different ways of communicating. We misunderstood one another right away. And in the absence of light there was darkness and in that darkness was fear. We never spoke to clear the air because that was not done in their family, so this made my doubts grow enormously. I needed resolution and clarity before I could move on back then. Basically, I needed a lot of reassurance. But one cannot give reassurance to another who is not assured of himself.

Forgiveness does not suggest that we forget, but rather it indicates that we are no longer willing to carry the pain for someone's actions. We release the anger and hurt. It is realizing that everyone around us is doing the best that they can for whom they are and the tools they have.

Lynn, a woman in class, shared that she was unable to move forward until she forgave her husband and herself for what they had created together. She saw herself constantly blaming her former husband for all that was negative in her present life. She felt this attitude of blame and anger held her back from creating anything positive in her life. They had no children and they did not have to be present in each other's lives, however she was stuck. Finally, the practice of forgiveness set her free. She saw her own powers at work in the creation of her marriage and focused her attention on herself and her needs during her relationship with her husband. Doing so, gave her enormous information about herself and the areas she needed to heal and release in order to create differently. Focusing her energy on herself allowed Lynn to heal and move forward. She had to release her husband in order to do this work.

Forgiveness can be a difficult step, but it is an important one because it does mean release. Why would we want to carry around with us the heaviness of hurt and anger over time? Doing so is like carrying heavy stones in our pockets, which makes every step we take more difficult and laborious. We need to lighten our loads and unburden ourselves, and forgiveness is a way to let go. If we are still holding onto the past, it takes away a lot of our power to create in the present. We still send a lot of mental energy to the past when we do not forgive and release our anger. Therefore, we are not fully and wholly here now.

One woman who was separated from her husband thirty-two years ago still held onto anger and hurt feelings toward him. They continued to raise three children, but never resolved their feelings toward one another. He died two years ago, and she realized she was *still* holding onto old emotions. She decided to look for what existed inside her that would attract that partner. Once she did this, she was able to accept responsibility for her part in creating the relationship with this partner. She could forgive him for his part in their relationship as well as herself. She had a better understanding of why he was whom he was when she looked at his upbringing. She finally had the ability to let go because she took another look at what she lived and her part in creating it. It opened the door for her to create differently in her life now. It is never too late to do this work.

It is relevant to reexamine the concept of compassion. When we look at ourselves and our partners and where we came from it is easier to understand the way we behave and communicate. We often refer to old maps of behavior to tell us how to live our lives. Our old maps are from our family of origin who molded us and formed the ways in which we were brought up. When we understand our choices and behaviors, we then have the opportunity to choose anew if old patterns no longer work for our

50

long-term goals. When we understand ourselves and our partners, we can then have compassion for both sides. We must realize the incomparable healing power of compassion. Others can benefit from our understanding. Compassion comes from accepting that we have done the best we can with the tools we have. If we have few tools it is harder to do intricate work. Relationships are similar. If we did not develop skills in communicating in our families, it is hard to conduct relationships later without the tools and training. Most of us did not develop these tools but we can learn and develop them. The possibilities are endless and limited only by our thinking.

During our mediation process, Jav and I were both caught up in a tornado of emotions. When I look back now, I understand so much more of what was happening between us and also individually. There was a painful moment when we were trying to settle the issue of child support. The mediators were asking my husband how much money he could afford monthly. Jav explained that his business was going bankrupt and alternated between being defensive and aggressive. It is clear to me now how men feel who are the primary wage earners in their families, when divorce occurs. Financial arrangements need to be determined. No one ever told Jav he was still needed in this family-- as a father, a friend and a co-parent. All that was asked of him was to show up for the financial portion.

Paul Ferrini, the renowned author wrote in his book, *Love Without Conditions,* "All anyone wants is to be loved and accepted as he/she is. Give him/her that, and she will have no need to attack you." As I reread my copy of his book, this passage struck me with its powerful message. If we can find our way back to love and accept each other, there would be no need to fight. I believe peace in the world starts in each and every home.

Divorce puts into question our sense of belonging, our value in the roles we have and (of course) love. It is difficult to be heart-centered and participate fully in providing for our children together when we are so lost in a sea of negative emotions. I think my husband felt lost and cast adrift. He was fearful and feeling unloved. Jav had terrible fears of losing his children. So did I. We were trying to settle intense financial issues in the middle of these strong emotions. There are often feelings of anger between partners separating, so there is very little desire to be generous either with money, time or material goods. This is because we operate from a place of fear. The fear is one of scarcity---that there is not enough of anything. Therefore, we have a tendency to hoard what we have. The fear and or anger are often manifested in the desire to see the other do without, even at the expense of the children.

A man courageously shared his story of withholding money from his former partner because of his anger toward her. He now understood that he was negatively affecting the lives of his children by engaging with his partner in this way. He stated he felt alone, as though his partner and his children were now a family unit without him and he was asked to support them financially. This made him angry and he adopted an attitude of, *you asked for this separation not me, let's see how you deal with the harsh reality.* This man went through a process of seeing himself anew and decided to create a vision for himself. He had to question who he was and who he wanted to be. He realized his own father had acted much the same as he had to divorce where finances were concerned. He witnessed his own mother struggling to support three children on a very low amount for child support. The question was never affordability, but the willingness to support both emotionally and financially, his family. This man decided to create differently. The situation was still challenging at times with his parenting partner, but he was very happy with whom he chose to be in his relationship with his children.

I believe that the process of divorce itself could use some re-creation. It felt void of care and validation. I now take responsibility for my fears at that moment, in that I looked to my husband to really help in the financial area just as he had in our marriage. I had old issues to deal with concerning money. I also had not worked in years and lacked confidence in my ability to support my children. I had expectations of who Jav would be and how he would respond to the situation. But he was not in a position to deal well then. Even if we do not get along in our marriages, we are still support for one another just by being present. Then we go through the process of separating out from one another and we no longer feel that base beneath us. In all of the instability, altered behavior is often apparent.

I suggest that we look anew at our intentions and those of our partners. There are moments when we act out and hurt our partners. Usually this is due to hurt and anger of our own. When we look at the full scope of a relationship, however, most people do not enter them with the intent to hurt the other. (If a relationship is truly abusive, we are dealing with much deeper issues). We enter relationships with the hope that we will be loved and give love. We intend to love fully, to give of ourselves. Our hearts are full of the beauty and wonder that is love. This is the *intent* and one must remember that this was alive in us and in our partners. Somewhere along the way, we lose sight of this wonder and we no longer feel loved. It is very powerful to recognize intent--both our own *and* our partners. Doing so helps to dissolve anger and hurt.

Assuming positive intentions often helps to omit angry reactions. Positive energy is lighter and leads to positive actions. Positive energy creates more positive energy, while negative forces perpetuate more negativity. Assuming the negative often leads to a snowballing of negative energy and doubt which then leads our minds on a downward facing path of reactions. Often the reactions we have are in response to something that has not actually occurred, but exists only in our anticipation of it. But our thoughts on the subject can help bring it to reality. An effective practice is the opposite, which is to act as if; act as if your partner of course, has good intentions and shared responsibility. Talk to them as if you see them this way. Visualize them this way as well as yourself. If we assume the positive we can act anew instead of re-acting in the same old ways. It is infusing a negative situation with new positive energy.

One woman shared that she was upset with the way her parenting partner shared responsibility with her. She felt he did not respond in a reasonable time frame to their child's needs such as new shoes or soccer gear, etc. They had agreed they would share costs as well as the actual errand to provide their children with whatever they needed. When it was his turn, she would remind him, but was frustrated when he would take 3-4 weeks to respond or not at all. We likened her reminders as taking responsibility for him as well as sounding like nagging to him. She did not like her role and realized that each time she called she anticipated his late response, which was evident in her speech to him. She decided to act anew and foresee a positive result. She knew that he had good intentions and did always take care of it but acknowledged organization was not his strong suit. By believing in him and sharing her belief with him, they both felt more positive from the beginning and while he did not respond immediately, it no longer took a month to take care of a need.

Another process that helped me was to allow myself to go back in time and let myself remember what it was like to be in love with my husband. I tried to remember our courtship. I started to remember what special things there were between us back then. I recalled my attraction to Jav's spirit and childlike joyfulness. He had a big heart and was a caring person. Jav was always generous with those he loved. I rediscovered an appreciation for these qualities in him now as a person in my life. I could release old expectations of him that I had when we were married and just accept him as he is. I had done a lot of work to be able to accept myself as I was. This sense of well being helps to let others be well too. I could love Jav and be his friend, but I did not have to own his behaviors or try to make him who he was not.

This affords us such tremendous freedom. All the responsibility that we put on ourselves for the other people in our lives is really too much to take on and yet, we do it so often. We take on the responsibility for everyone's happiness. If everyone is not happy than we appoint ourselves responsible for changing that. This can be an enormous burden that we choose to carry. In reality, all we owe anyone else is to be well ourselves. We set a great example just by being ourselves. We are not responsible for everyone's experience, but we are responsible for respecting others' experiences just as we do our own.

It is stunning to really look at the power of love. Right now I am witnessing my mother falling in love at the age of sixty-five. She is radiant and so full of joy and anticipation. Love is affording her safety for the first time in her life to look back and deal with some big issues she has always held onto regarding her mother. Her mother died when she was seventeen and they never had a close relationship. My mother never felt loved and celebrated by her mother. She has nursed hurt and anger all her life. This has been present in every one of her subsequent relationships. It has also manifested greatly in her physical health. Yet, now with this person showing her love and helping her to see her own beauty as a person, she has the security to look back without fear. She has developed enough love for herself and her friend that she is now able to extend love, compassion and forgiveness to her mother for the first time. For the first time in my life, my mother shared a positive memory about her mother. Love gives us this. It fills us up so we have abundance, enough to share with all those around us. Seeing our own beauty settles our hearts and lets us know that all is well. Sometimes this comes by seeing ourselves reflected in another. Eventually, we have to own this all on our own. We need to love ourselves just as we are, to fill ourselves up with love regardless of a romantic partner's presence.

It is important to remember the moments of love that we shared and that we created together. We invite people into our lives for reasons. I believe that everyone comes bearing gifts. We need to create certain life experiences to get to where we want to go, to help us remember who we are and why we came here. There are lessons to be learned, most of them about ourselves. If we turn our backs on everything that we have created with others because the relationship ended or it was painful, we will not receive the gifts of that experience. If we do not open ourselves up to the experience in its entirety, we are not opening up to our own self. When we speak in demeaning tones about another in a relationship, we demean ourselves as well and this leads to more diminishing thoughts and actions but not concerning the other, just ourselves. It is time to be aware of what we wish to give ourselves in every thought as well as deed. It is important to look back with gratitude for the people who passed through our lives and shared a dance with us, because they have taught us well about whom we are. I once thought that my mother-in-law was my enemy; now I see her as an angel who taught me so much about my belief in myself. I needed her to mirror me to allow me to see that I was not being the grandest version of the vision I held of myself. If we are not well in our skins we will invite others into our lives who are not well. Just as anger attracts anger, victims attract victims. You will find that what is going on in your emotions often actualizes in your life. This is true of people with whom we create relationships.

My daughter, Bronte, has been asking me repeatedly if I still love her father. My answer has always been yes, but in a different way than when we were married. She would reply that her daddy says he loves me in the *same* way as always. This difference in our answers clearly bothered her. After months of this discussion, I realized that I was dissecting, analyzing and classing something that cannot be measured. I needed to pay attention to the message my daughter was giving me. All that really matters, is that yes, of course, I still love Jav. And I always will love him. The beauty and simplicity of this made me still for a moment. The most important element is the existence of love. Only through my daughter's clarity could I understand and release all of the complications I was placing upon the quality of love I felt for Jav.

GETTING BACK TO A PLACE OF LOVE EXERCISE

1.   Are you still angry or blaming your partner?

_____

_____

_____

_____

2.   Are you willing to let this go? How will this change your life? What are you gaining by not letting this go?

_____

_____

_____

_____

3.   Look again at how you were co-creating your relationship. List the ways you helped to create this.

_____

_____

_____

4.   Practice seeing your partner's background (how they were raised), and living life through their perspective. In what ways can you better understand their actions, decisions and ways of communicating based on where they came from?

_____

_____

_____

_____

5. What can you gain by developing compassion for yourself and your partner? What can you lose by never feeling this compassion?

_____

_____

_____

_____

_____

6. What did it feel like to be in love with your partner? Paint a picture here of the beginning of your relationship together. What did you fulfill for each other?

_____

_____

_____

_____

_____

7. Practice a forgiveness ritual. Visualize your partner and see him/her as perfect, whole and complete. Release the past. Also, see yourself as perfect, whole and complete. Release the past.

_____

_____

_____

_____

_____

_____

_____

CHAPTER 7

CREATING CHANGE NEEDS SUPPORT

Divorce is pervasively viewed as negative in our society. I had a negative view of divorce, in part, from living through it as a child. When my parents divorced in 1969, it was not a good thing. My mother was considered crazy for leaving an upstanding all-American guy such as my father. She was not happy; my father was an alcoholic, albeit a successful professional. Their intimate life together was not healthy or fulfilling, so she chose to leave the marriage. My mother's family was horrified by this and sided against her in favor of my father. Divorce is still considered negative today due to the often, devastating effects it has on families. In order to re-create our families we must release old labels and mind-sets and re-create in positive ways to sustain ourselves and our families.

Much of the judgment toward divorce stems from an attachment to form and arbitrary numbers. We have collectively agreed that long-term marriages are better than short-term marriages. We assume couples married for 20-50 years (regardless of being fulfilled or happy) are much more admirable and respectable than couples married for a shorter time. Society often values relationships based on age as opposed to content and meaning. I reiterate: A relationship is not diminished in value due to its ending. When a marriage ends, it does not in any way preclude a meaningful relationship between the two people involved. In fact, quite the contrary is possible if we care to see or accept the unlimited opportunities. There is rich knowledge of one another that comes from loving and sharing life together. This knowledge can be used to support rather than hurt one another, but the choice is ours. The choice leads back to setting your intention of whom you want to be and what you would like to create.

A crucial part of creating change is support. Creating change requires commitment, attention and focus. It also needs a great support group. During my separation, my sister Kelly, shared with me her feelings toward Jav. She told me she was very angry with him, so much so that there were moments she felt violently toward him. That was an incredible level of anger for Kelly. There was resentment toward him from my family, who witnessed my escalating pain. When this happens, we usually want to appoint someone responsible. Similarly, Jav's family had anger and strong feelings toward me. People often seek reinforcement for their feelings while expressing blame and anger. We most need someone however, to just listen to us pour out our big feelings of hurt, anger and fear. The danger of getting other people involved is that we often move on and let go, while the other person has a difficult time abandoning his/her investment in the problem.

It is crucial to have a support system around us in life. It is equally important to ask for the kind of encouragement we want. In order to decide what we want, we must revisit our intention that we set. We need to share this with our support team. It helped my sister and my mother to let go of their feelings when they saw what Jav and I were creating together. They saw our ability to move forward and how this affected our family. Positive energy was being created. Positive energy creates more positive energy and negative energy multiplies exponentially as well. Which do you choose to live with everyday? My family and friends moved forward because that is where I chose to lead. We collectively decided not to embrace the past, but to set it free. In doing so, we set ourselves free. I told my family where I wanted to go with my parenting partner and my children. They, in turn, always recognized the strides I made and encouraged my efforts. My friends have done the same for me throughout the last five years. Even when my choices differed from their opinions, they celebrated my progress. It would have been a much longer road without their help and support.

One man shared his story of support. He belongs to a men's group specifically supporting each other in developing their vision of themselves. He has been divorced for a number of years, but has steadfastly devoted time, emotional support and financial support to his children and his former partner. He has since remarried and has had another child, but remains devout in his

60

support of his children and parenting partner. There is never a question in his mind of his turn or her turn, instead he adopts an attitude that says if it is something for his children, he is willing to help, always. He consistently, takes responsibility for his part in his family and dedicates himself to being the father he aspires to be. His men's group is a great source of support for creating the vision he has for himself.

I feel very strongly about making every effort to speak positively about parenting partners. There are moments when this is challenging because anger and disappointment arise, and yet it helps nothing to have a session of insults about them or with them. Doing so only further entrenches us in negative feelings. This is not to say we cannot have these feelings, but I advocate clearing them with the person involved or doing some release work on ourselves. In the long run, directly addressing the problem is more beneficial than speaking disparagingly about our parenting partner. Try letting anger out in a safe way by yelling, using a punching bag or hitting the bed. Exorcising the anger and establishing a sense of calm is essential in resolving problems between the individuals involved. Through trial and error, I have found that when I have a problem with my children's father, it is best to discuss it with him during a calm moment when I am centered. We have worked out a communication code that says we have feelings to share. We still might take time to get to a mutual answer, but we are putting in the time to negotiate calmly. Jav and I still hit emotional moments as we come to new territory in our lives sharing our children. Our goal now seems to be open communication between him, his wife and myself with whatever comes up in the family. We are trying to be compassionate with one another as new situations arise and to be considerate of each other and ourselves.

Positive support is needed in all areas, including mass media. I read a column where people write to a magazine for advice from professionals. These professionals often call the people names or belittle them in other ways for their behavior and their choices. One woman wrote a popular magazine that espouses positive attitudes. She wrote about needing help with her ex-husband because of her anger toward him and his new girlfriend. She was belittling the child's father due to her anger at him. The advice columnist was so harsh to this woman. I remember being so upset that this woman, who was crying out for help, was being treated with a punishing attitude by the therapist writing in response to her. It was amazing to me that this courageous woman was demeaned when she exposed her unlovable parts. This woman was not given compassion in her demand for help. How can we help others more effectively without publicly humiliating them? This woman probably will not go back and help her daughter see her father with love, because she was not given any. We can do better than this for ourselves. A man wrote to a divorce magazine asking for help and he was called, a "loser" by the columnist for his willingness to share his doubt about himself. How can this treatment possibly help? When people ask for advice they are seeking a way to ease their pain or unhappiness. It seems to be entertaining to see people being publicly slaughtered. We all deserve better treatment; we need to create such an environment together.

We still need good communication tools when we are no longer married just as we do when we are married, perhaps even more so. Married people can engage in prolonging their disputes, because it often does not disrupt their daily life. This is not the case, however, when we are in two homes. We need to resolve immediate issues of finances, pick-ups, drop-offs, vacations, family events, etc. Thus, we really need effective communication skills when dealing with our parenting partners. These skills are an integral part of facilitating and negotiating win-win outcomes.

I noticed that my parenting partner could still push my buttons and make me react immediately either with anger or defensiveness. This halted our communication right away, and we often took 1-2 weeks to arrive at an agreement on any given issue. Therefore, we had residual emotions in every conversation thereafter. I spoke to my Uncle Terry, who is my mentor and a spiritual practitioner. He offered me a great insight. He said that while Jav pushed my buttons *I*, initially programmed my buttons and, therefore, was solely able to re-program them. I was stuck in a mode of feeling out of control with my emotions when my partner attacked with anger and accusations. All my insecurities came flying to the forefront to deny or to defend, which is what I did when I was married. I realized that when someone was angry with me, I did not feel loved and this produced fear in me. So I would desperately try to remedy whatever came up regardless of who's problem it was. When I spoke to my uncle, I realized I could help myself feel in charge by not re-acting to Jav anymore. I could choose another action altogether. This was a helpful application in my life with every relationship. This is simple, but it is not easy. Practice is a necessity.

I then stopped re-acting to Jav's emotions, whatever they were. I learned to listen and validate Jav, regardless of the reasons behind his anger. Everyone just wants to be heard, and Jav was no different. My validation had a calming effect on him. If I owned the problem, I could apologize and if not, I could use questions to help him find a solution. I realized that anger directed at me always made me nervous, but I did not have to be uncomfortable anymore. I am responsible for my feelings, but not for Jav's. This understanding was key in helping me to stay calm. Therefore, problems did not escalate as they did in the past.

One man shared that the way his parenting partner spent money drove him crazy, and he could not stop himself from making derisive remarks about it. He admitted that he felt afraid that if she mismanaged her money, he would end up being responsible for her. When he realized he was still holding onto old re-actions, he was able to choose new ones consciously. When he next visited her and noticed (unnecessary) new furniture in her house, he complimented her on it instead. He let her assume responsibility for her choices. When he used his new *action* mode instead of *re-action*, he had a much better moment with his partner. He also gave himself peace, in that he was no longer re-acting out of fear that he was responsible. He learned to let go.

There was an amazing moment in my life last year when I came across the books of Neale Donald Walsch. Walsch is the acclaimed author of the *Conversations With God* book series. I read all of his books within two months and then attended a New Year's retreat, led by Walsch, with my sister. It was life altering in that it gave me renewed faith in who I was and in what I had created in my family for the past four years. Walsch shared his view that deciding who you are is *remembering* who you are and *being* that. He then expressed that what a person does comes from who he/she is. Another part of the lesson entailed being who you are no matter the setting in which you find yourself. Walsch warned the group that when one declares who one is, often the opposite emerges. This was true for myself. I decided that I was love and light. During that year, I had a big break in a friendship with a close friend. Even though I had been working toward the creation of this material, I went into a cave of doubt. I doubted whether or not I was capable of actually doing this work. The year held incredible insights for me. Still, I was determined to get back to being me and letting go of fear and doubt. My support group of friends and family was instrumental in helping me to remember who I was and believe in my own ability to create what I wanted. They helped me to see my own beauty and celebrate me. This reinforced the passionate feelings I had about re-creating families after divorce.

When you decide to be different in your family, there will be a reaction. If at first the response is not positive, give it time. Change can make us feel uncomfortable. Think of a moment when someone you know changed and how you reacted to that change. What would happen if that person were no longer the person you have always known? And yet, what if you decided to look forward to the new emerging person with enthusiasm? In any case, there will most likely be a response in your family to the change in you. It will take time for the positive attitude to take effect and bring positive results. Let the response come. Try to be patient; everyone is shifting and trying to find a rhythm. We need to commit ourselves to being who we want to be and lead from our hearts, regardless of the setting around us. These are powerful lessons.

One woman shared that people around her noticed a difference in her and asked her what she was doing, because she seemed different to them. They noticed she was truly well and had balance in her life. This showed in the way she held herself and reacted to everyone around her. She was still going through a difficult time re-creating her family, however she had a vision and was working toward it now. She shared that a big part of her success was the fact that she was asking and receiving support to create her vision. Even her former partner asked her what she was doing, because he noticed a positive change in her.

We all need support in life. This chapter is about asking for the support to do what we want. It feels overwhelming when we separate or isolate ourselves and feel as though we have to do everything on our own. It takes a community to raise our children. Look to the schools for support in helping our children. Dialogue with teachers to encourage our children to be all they can be. The women in my workshop developed the idea of speaking to the teachers in our community school and asking them for positive support at the beginning of the year when children are asked to describe their families. The women wanted to ask the teachers to promote the awareness that families come in all kinds of wonderful packages. They do not all look alike, but they are all families. This kind of dialogue can help free children to be comfortable with where they come from and celebrate it. This view, coming from the classroom as well as the home, can be a very powerful support for our children as well as ourselves. We can also invite other family members (in) to help support our efforts. I have two wonderful uncles who are committed to participating in my family and helping me with my children. They are another avenue of love and support for me and my kids. My sister and my mother are incredibly participatory in my family. My mother commits to spending time with my children every Thursday night, enabling me to attend yoga. This offers me some rejuvenation and gives them some quality time together. Look at the people around you and invite them in. I guarantee you people yearn to feel valued, loved and as though they belong. People in your situation can be another avenue of support. Swap baby-sitting to take a class or to get in your self-care time. There are many ways to get help and support, but you need to be willing to ask for it. I spent years feeling overwhelmed by the weight and responsibility of my circumstances until I realized help is all around me, but I did not ask for it. That was my choice, but I can always choose again if I wish to change things. We can adopt change if situations are not working for us. We can have love and support in our lives. We all deserve that.

I know of a woman who exemplifies the benefits that can be attained when one asks for much needed support. She calls her good friend whenever she needs a positive mind-set for her day or her life challenge at that moment. She calls as often as she needs, always asking first if it is a good time and then discusses her problems. She sets up the scenario and quickly states where she wants to get to from there. The friend can then help guide her in that direction. Sometimes, we just need that extra help to get where we want to go. This woman also reciprocates to her friend when her friend needs it. Thus, they both benefit from the positive support.

In sum, we need to reevaluate our views on divorce and how it impacts our families. Do we continue to harbor negative views about our situations? How can we turn these around and embrace both who we are and our family circumstances? The best way is by creating the vision of yourself and your family. In order to make your vision a reality, we need support and encouragement to stay focused on our path.

CREATING CHANGE NEEDS SUPPORT EXERCISE

1. What kind of changes would you like to create in your family relationships?

_____

_____

_____

_____

_____

2. What kind of support would you like to have?

_____

_____

_____

3. Is it difficult for you to ask for support? What are you gaining by not asking for support? What might you gain by getting the support you desire? What might your children gain?

_____

_____

_____

_____

_____

4. Are there people in your life who you can ask for support?

_____

_____

_____

5. Are there any local groups you can join?

_____

_____

_____

_____

6. Can you start your own support group? Who might you ask
to participate?

_____

_____

_____

_____

7. Do you make efforts to speak positively about your parenting
partner? If not why?

_____

_____

_____

8. Do you need new communication tools for interaction with
your children and/or your parenting partner? Are there
parenting classes available near you?

_____

_____

_____

_____

_____

_____

_____

9. What are your views on divorce? If they are negative, what can you do to make your family story into something positive?

_____

_____

_____

_____

_____

10. Does your parenting partner still have the power to push your buttons? If so, what can you do to re-program your buttons?

_____

_____

_____

_____

_____

_____

_____

_____

_____

_____

_____

_____

_____

_____

_____

CHAPTER 8

LETTING YOUR CHILDREN KNOW

It is vital to have clear communication with your children during this time of change in your lives. They need to know what is happening in their family so that they have comfort in knowing what to expect. They are also very intuitive people, and they know when things are well and when they are not. Being truthful with your children will help create a trusting relationship between all of you as a family. They will know that they can rely on their parents to prepare them with whatever information is necessary.

The first step is acknowledging the changes that have occurred in their lives. This might be their home changing and mom or dad moving out. I chose to tell them we could not be peaceful and calm in the same house, so we chose to live apart. I reaffirmed that we would always be there to take care of them. I told them that somewhere in our hearts we still had love for each other, but we needed time to calm down. Then I started sharing the story of our beginning and the beginning of their lives. I related how we celebrated their arrivals and how much we wanted them.

A woman in class shared her resistance to sharing with her children what was happening in their lives. It felt final and it felt negative to her. Saying it out loud to her children made her afraid even though she could not remain with her husband of many years. Her kids were close to teens and had knowledge of what was happening. She realized a lot of her fear came from the fact that her husband wanted to remain together and she felt guilt about leaving the marriage which made her avoid speaking of it to her children. Once she acknowledged her fear and its source she was able to understand it better and make a plan for speaking openly and honestly with her children about their divorce and the subsequent changes in their lives.

People always want to be loved, valued and feel they belong. Divorce can feel like a huge rupture, because these feelings are in question. We can encourage our children that we believe in them and their ability to flourish. It is my priority to be fully present and wish my children a good time when they leave to spend time with their dad. This is to let my children know that I believe they can be well during the time without me. This also reinforces their belief in themselves. It gives them the freedom to enjoy and to love their father without guilt. Brontë and Niky know when I leave them that I am well. They also know that I support the time they spend with their father. My support gives them the freedom to live and to love.

We were having a difficult time during our separation and, therefore, so were our children. My daughter, Brontë, did not display any distress signs, because she was just one year-old. On the other hand, my four-year-old son, Niky, actively displayed his anguish. He would come home from his visits with his father and pace in the garden for twenty minutes screaming "No!" His father was feeling quite lost and having a hard time saying goodbye to the children without tears. I felt the same, and we were both trying to find safety and help our children. Children are intuitive creatures. They know exactly what is happening even if they cannot verbalize it. Verbal communication is one of the most primitive forms of communication. It is the form, however, on which we most rely. Our little people have no filters. They can read emotions in a room and know whether things are well. Kids can also receive emotions from adults. This is one of the important reasons to be honest with your children about what is happening in both your lives and their lives. Somewhere in their beings, they already know. You are confirming their trust in their own emotions and intuition.

I chose to let my son scream, and I was company for him while he let it out. This was not easy. It was often scary and frustrating when his big feelings would take on a destructive nature. I would then employ limits, while encouraging Niky to let out his feelings. I also chose to let both my children know, in terms they could understand, why their mom and dad were no longer living together.

It is always best to keep details private between the two people involved in the relationship. Barring the presence of danger for yourself and your children, it is too much for children to know all the details of our adult relationships. We are bigger than life to young children and even to some adolescents. They do not understand the workings of adult relationships because they do not make things as complicated as we do. Children love unconditionally. If they are aware of too many details (as we perceive them) they often feel as though they must choose sides. And this is a terrible position in which to place a child. When put in this place it is unsafe for a child to love because sharing love with one parent can hurt the other parent. Imagine how this affects kids when they become adults, knowing from a young age that it is unsafe to show love due to the risk of hurting someone else.

Children are very willing to take responsibility for us as their parents if that is what we ask of them. That does not mean they deserve that burden. It can become so encompassing that they cannot live out their childhood and adolescence, which can delay their development socially and emotionally. Once again this is about taking responsibility for what we have created. Using our children as friends and confidants robs them of their childhood, forces them to take sides, and makes them partners in hurt and blame.

After we had moved, I started telling my son the story of his birth. I told him how happy we were when we found out he was coming. I told him this story because it helped me feel attached to the beauty of our past and it helped my son to know there was love even when it felt as though the opposite was true. The story of Niky's birth became his favorite and led to other tales of how his mom and dad met. I now realize this was a gift to myself. Reconfirming these tender emotions was healing, even though as a couple, my husband and I were saying "goodbye" to each other.

We can share with children the story of our love and how they are the product of our love. My children love to hear anecdotes about both their parents growing up and our married days. I think Jav found it touching when he found me telling boyhood stories that were shared in his family about him. My children love it and it made him feel celebrated within the family. Knowing their origin is very grounding to our children. If you cannot find anything positive to share with your children, then step back from engaging in this practice. This exercise is not to be forced. The goal is to develop an appreciation for your past marriage partner. If you need time to release old feelings onto which you have been holding, just acknowledge they exist and set an intention to let them go. It is quite a powerful application.

A woman in class shared that her decision to share her story of love with her children had a positive effect on them. She chose to put pictures of herself and her former partner together in her children's rooms. She has noticed that her children feel comforted by this rather than confused. They know exactly where they came from and understand the story of their parents lives together (though not the details).

As my children have grown, so has their need for more information about their parents. These moments become intense as they share strong feelings of wanting their parents to be together again. Jav and I learned by experience that our children benefit when we share a broad picture of why we separated and omit the details. I tell them that over the years I stopped feeling loved in our marriage and I helped to create that feeling myself. I tell my children I now know their parents loved each other. This is my truth simple as it sounds, and it seems to be enough for them right now.

Over the years Jav and I tried it another way and found things to be very difficult. My son once became very heated toward his dad and demanded a reason for why we were not together. Jav, I think, felt very cornered and said he had tried to get back together and mom refused. My son came home with a set of strong feelings toward me. He absolutely exploded and demanded to know why I would not let his dad come home. Niky was understandably angry and he had a right to his feelings. He had just been given a target for his anger at his parent's choices. In short, he had someone to blame. Javi had unknowingly made me the villain, and we now both understood to consider carefully what we shared with our children. Jav has every right to his feelings toward me due to the decision I made, but he also needs to take responsibility for those feelings. We decided to have a family meeting for my son's sake to discuss what Jav had said and Niky's subsequent reaction. We told our children that we heard their wishes. It gave us all a lot to think about. It was a good learning experience.

The goal of this chapter is to help us realize that our children must still feel they are part of a family. They are loved and they are valued. In order to give this to our children, however, we must first create this love and value for ourselves. We cannot give what we do not have to offer. If you feel the best way to help your children, is through help spiritually or emotionally, then seek that assistance. There are great therapists and spiritual practitioners who can help facilitate this process. If we are not well, we cannot take good care of our children. We cannot start on this journey for only their sake -- it must be for us. We deserve ultimate well being and from this our children will benefit. When we can accept ourselves and our marriage partners with love and compassion we can truly show our children the way by example. We can set our children free to be their wonderful selves, to give and receive love.

LETTING YOUR CHILDREN KNOW EXERCISE

1. What have you told your children about the changes in your family?

_____

_____

_____

_____

_____

_____

_____

2. If you have avoided doing so, list your reasons why.

_____

_____

_____

_____

_____

_____

_____

If fear is hindering you from apprising your children of your family's situation, do the following exercise. Visualize yourself telling your children the truth. What fear surfaces? Then ask yourself: What if that fear comes true? Continue questioning "what if" as each new fear/thought arises, until you reach the core of your fears. Remember by exposing our deepest fear we take away its power over us and thereby, empower ourselves to state our truth and help our children heal.

Practice here what you can tell your children about the changes occurring within your family without laying blame.

3. Are you sharing too much information with your children about your relationship with your parenting partner? If so, what is your goal in doing this? How is it affecting your children?

_____

_____

_____

_____

_____

_____

_____

4. How can you help to make the transition from one parent to the other happen more smoothly? What can you model for your parenting partner?

_____

_____

_____

_____

_____

_____

_____

_____

_____

_____

_____

_____

CHAPTER 9

HONORING YOUR CHILDREN'S FEELINGS AND YOUR OWN

I discovered early on that my children would have their own feelings about our divorce, regardless of what I did. In the beginning, I tried everything to smooth the way for my children. This took many forms and most of them came from guilt. I felt I owed my children so much for having chosen something, which upended their lives. I was not with someone who beat me or who was a terrible person and yet I was terribly unhappy. I struggled to determine whether I had sufficient cause to take action and make changes in my life. Were my feelings *alone* enough to subject my family to a process that would undoubtedly be painful and profoundly affect us?

Although I had known for some time that our family would not improve, I was reticent to leave my marriage, as I doubted the relative importance of my happiness. I finally became clear when I saw myself physically and emotionally unwell. I then realized that if I sacrificed my own happiness to stay in a "family" setting, I would soon experience some serious health issues. I could no longer deny that ending our marriage was my only solution. This realization created enormous concerns regarding how my children and their father would be impacted. Even though my love for my husband had changed, I still felt incredibly resistant to sharing my feelings with him, because I did not want him to be hurt. I felt guilty for changing my children's lives with their father. Basically, I now know I felt responsible for everyone's happiness. I find this to be a very feminine (but not exclusive to women) response in that women regularly take on responsibility for the happiness of those around them.

Feelings of guilt about my separation led me to over parent my children. I was *still* helping my son pick out his clothes and get dressed when he was seven. I continually saved my children from experiencing ordinary life and its natural consequences. In essence, I prevented my kids from taking responsibility for

77

themselves and their actions. When I became conscious of all this, I started making changes. I realized my mistake when I recognized my children's emotional immaturity due to my over-parenting and over-protective attitude. I gradually stepped back and allowed my children to come forward. I took a great parenting class and set an intention for my parenting, which I still work on everyday. Old habits are hard to break and new habits take time to forge. Awareness was the first step for me.

I had to become aware of the guilt I carried and how it dictated my mode of parenting. This is when I read the work of a great author named Louise Hay. She is a world-renowned spiritual healer. She wrote the book "You Can Heal Your Life". It helped me to honestly get in touch with myself to clarify my issues. When I started to recognize what my issues were, Hay's book enabled me to more clearly understand the dynamics of my marriage. The marriage that Jav and I created was a product of who we were *then*. Recognizing why I had certain needs and fears helped me to release them and to move forward. I had to release the guilt over my choice to leave my husband. I had to get to a place where it was safe to celebrate my choice and know that I deserved my consideration. This required much work. Giving up the guilt allowed me to be present for parenting and leading my own life, instead of trying to satisfy an unpayable debt. I model for my children how to care for myself and to believe that everyone is worthy of love. I could not do that while I was in my marriage.

When my son, Niky, would share his angry feelings about our family situation I shouldered complete responsibility for his feelings, thereby feeding my guilt. This behavior taught my son that I was responsible for any and all of his negative feelings. I was inadvertently fixing everything for Niky. I did not give him the belief that he was capable of doing what he needed or wanted. The result was anger---and that anger was directed toward me. Continually taking responsibility for a child's feelings can cripple his/her emotional and social development.

78

When my children express anger or frustration over our living arrangements, I use reflective listening skills and allow their feelings to be their experience at that moment. In order to employ reflective listening skills, I repeat what the children have said in my own words, to let them know I have heard them and understand their words. They have feelings that arise when they say goodbye to their dad for a few days. I have come to realize is that this is okay. My children simply need me to validate their experience. Sometimes, it does feel bad or sad to say goodbye and it is best to express it. However, if I can make it safe for them to express their emotions without owning them myself, then they truly have the opportunity to work through these feelings. What we most want when we are upset is to be heard. I find I can now listen without owning their feelings, and this benefits our communication. Expressing our emotions enables us to release, rather than repress them.

One woman in class, who recently divorced from her husband, had two teenage children. She realized her kids were having a difficult time adjusting to the upheaval and change that was now evident in their lives. She chose to support her kids by opening the door for their communication with her and letting them know it was safe to express their emotions even if those emotions felt negative. Receiving the message that it was safe to speak, these kids then gave voice to their emotions and upset over their situation. They now have a better chance of dealing with their hurt being vocal, rather than silent and repressing their emotions.

Another mother had a son who was reacting quite negatively to her divorce from his father. He became angry and sided with his father in blame, having been exposed to adult matters between his parents. This mother chose to respect her son's wishes to remain distant from her, however, she e-mailed him daily supporting him in his life choices and letting him know how loved he was by her. She steadfastly remained loyal to her son and her love for him, and waited. Her son has finally responded to her devout support and they are re-creating their relationship together.

Children who are older experiencing their parents' divorce, often feel angry over the changes in their lives. As we grow older we learn to form attachments to the way things are. This makes accepting change much more difficult. Teens are frequently worried about how they will appear to others around them. Despite the fact that 50% of marriages end in divorce, kids still feel as though they are the only ones going through this experience. They feel isolated and exhibit mood swings, from anger to sullen silence, to sadness. It is vital to have open communication within a family, to air feelings and allow them to be released. Younger children experiencing divorce often act out their fears about the changes in their lives. Because younger children live truly in the moment they adapt and adjust more rapidly than teens. That is not to suggest that they are not affected because they are. Adopting good parenting and communication tools, however, help support these children tremendously.

If you feel reactive when your children are going through their own release or venting, try to note your response in an observing way without judging yourself. Keep breathing through the moment and allow your child his/her opportunity to share emotions with kind, yet, firm limits. Revisit your feelings when you can give yourself a quiet moment of reflection. While noting the feelings that have arisen, pinpoint the cause of these emotions. Was your child's tone of voice or demeanor the catalyst for your feelings? Were you reactive to the subject being discussed? Try to remember not to judge your child or yourself. Doing so forges a new habit of being kind to yourself. You are not at fault for having feelings. Feelings are neutral, how you manage your feelings is key. When your children have anger toward you as a parent, do *you* become angry and defensive? Can you allow your children to get angry and teach them the appropriate skills to express that emotion? Likewise, are you helpful to your children when they are upset with your co-parent or do you exacerbate the problem due to your own negative feelings regarding your former partner? Carefully examining such issues is integral to envisioning your goal, setting an intention and re-creating yourself.

When my children were very young I felt no one could take care of them as well as I. This was evident in my controlling and belittling attitude regarding my co-parents participation. I judged myself harshly and therefore, I did the same to my partner. I realized I was denying my children's right to experience their father and their sense of self. I could give them the gift of believing in themselves and having the confidence to deal with whatever happened. I believe that our children choose us as their parents to help provide the perfect backdrop for whatever they would like to explore in this lifetime. My children have a divine right to experience their father in his entirety, just as they do their mother. Throughout their lives, my children will decide what they would like to do with the information and role-modeling Jav and I provide.

What I now give my children when they feel anger is a place to voice their feelings and state what would work for them. It is a matter of negotiating and compromising. I also encourage them to speak to their father about any feelings they have toward him or an experience with him. He is then able to deal with these issues as he feels best. I still struggle with letting him be who he is even if he might sound too punishing or passive to me at times. My goal is to stop judging Jav and myself. My goal is to get to a place of acceptance. I am not advocating a passive response if a child is in danger or being demeaned within a family. If you feel in your heart this is happening I suggest professional help to assist gaining appropriate parenting tools.

Being a guide for a child is one of the biggest jobs any of us will ever have in life. There is very little training or preparation for the job. Parenting classes are tremendously advantageous because they help us develop new communication tools and to define our parenting roles. Actually our children are the best guides and all we have to do is pay attention to that which we have forgotten. Notice your children's unconditional love for you. Appreciate their ability to let go of things and to move on to the next moment. Note how children ask for what they want. Celebrate how they naturally give and receive love. We can all practice these things more in our daily lives.

Overall I have learned to check in with myself to see how I am feeling toward others or regarding certain situations. This is a learned skill for me, because I did not always trust or honor how I felt. It was not the way I was taught. This is not a statement of blame, just a fact. Once I recognized the importance of identifying and gauging my emotions, I was free to change aspects of my situation. There are still occasions that cause me to question how I feel and identify those emotions.

This process of identifying my feelings proved helpful when Jav requested the children accompany him and Ingrid, his girlfriend to visit her parents in San Francisco. The first time he asked me two years ago, I reacted indignantly. I became all worked up and rationalized that Jav being from Mexico should not spend the holiday with the children as he did not celebrate it until we were married. As he was not then married to Ingrid I felt absolute in my decision that the children should be with me. I now realize the profound fear I had of Niky and Brontë being gone at that time. Fear can make us act out in many ways. Javi asked to spend Thanksgiving with the children again this year and although nothing has changed, I have. I was still fearful of letting go, but I decided to send them with good wishes for a fun time. Being without my kids during a holiday for the first time was challenging and provoked tears. However, permitting my children to go became a positive personal experience rather than one of loss. I gained faith that I would be fine and able to create a moment for myself that is joyful. Admittedly though, even when Javi asked to take kids the second time, I had to sit for a few days and truly evaluate my feelings. It is healthy to give ourselves these moments of pause to see where we are. Ask your partner and your children for these moments and get back to them with a thoughtful response. Try to be flexible in working out solutions that work for everyone.

When we are struggling in life, it is often more important to look at ourselves at this point. What are we holding onto so tightly? Frequently, we become so invested in a particular outcome that there is no other possible way. By surrendering our position or following the current, we can help reclaim our energy toward enjoying what is here and now rather than continuing to fight toward an outcome we have decided is the only one acceptable. When we flow with the current of the river instead of swimming against it, we can actually notice all that is happening around us – float on our backs and enjoy the scenery.

I have learned that feelings are neither, bad nor good they are *neutral*. What we do with those feelings matters greatly. Our choices stem from the intentions we set for ourselves. Our feelings are derived from our thoughts and a thought can be changed. We must be aware of our emotions and step back from judging them. The next time negative feelings arise, try to notice what is happening with your body, breath and thoughts. Pause then for a moment and experience the uncomfortable feelings. Doing this facilitates the release of these emotions. Valuable information about ourselves is revealed through this process. Once we learn how to process these feelings we can teach this to our children. The core of this chapter is to allow ourselves and our children to experience our individual feelings and adopt tools with which to express these emotions. Refraining from judging our feelings is tremendously liberating and is a prerequisite to achieving acceptance.

HONORING YOUR CHILDREN'S FEELINGS AND YOUR OWN EXERCISE

1. How do you feel when your children express feelings about your divorce? living situation? parenting partner?

    _____

    _____

    _____

    _____

    _____

    _____

2. Do you continue to feel guilt about your decisions regarding your divorce? How does this guilt affect your life?

    _____

    _____

    _____

    _____

3. What would happen if you let go of the guilt in your life? What benefits would you experience?

    _____

    _____

    _____

    _____

    _____

Create a vision of how you would like to respond to your children when they express their feelings. Let love guide you. What would love do now?

4. What do you need to release or change from your answer to #1 to create your vision?

_____

_____

_____

_____

_____

_____

5. Do you feel you could benefit by taking a parenting class? Gaining new tools of communication with your children? Learning how to set limits that are respectful to everyone?

_____

_____

_____

_____

_____

_____

_____

_____

_____

_____

_____

_____

_____

_____

_____

CHAPTER 10

NEW LABELS AND NEW PARTNERS

Language is a powerful tool and how we choose to use it is decidedly influential. We can employ labels and words that describe our family and ourselves in ways that evoke either good or bad feelings. After Jav and I separated, I explored the negative feelings I had attached to certain phrases. I did not use the word "divorce" with my children for four years, because it did not feel good. I stayed away from "ex-husband", as well. When I would speak of my children's father, I just called him "Jav" as though everyone would know whom I meant. "Ex-husband" felt like I was ex-ing him out of my life which made me uncomfortable. There were moments when I was angry with him and wanted no further contact. When I realized this was unrealistic and we would surely share a future raising our children, I began to create a vision.

I questioned once again who I wanted to be and what I wanted for my family. My family would be greatly affected by whom I was. The old labels did not work for me, so I chose or created new ones. I am not saying that old labels are bad, but they felt bad to me. I recommend using words and labels that celebrate what you are creating in your family. Employ terms that evoke positive feelings. This might initially sound superficial until you note the feelings you have after describing your family negatively. Compare the difference in your feelings after using positive terminology. For example, experience the feelings evoked when someone utters the term "broken family." Now compare the emotions conjured by the phrase "two home family." The first example sounds very negative and will provoke a negative emotional feeling, while the second sounds neutral and states a truth. One may go further and simply call themselves a family. Doing so is the most celebratory way to label any family. Over time, our feelings have a powerful effect on how we view our family and our role in it.

When Javier became involved in a serious relationship with Ingrid (now his wife), we all went through a change. There was now a new partner for Jav and a new parent figure for the children. I questioned how I would want to interact with Ingrid. The relationship could be anything I wanted. Given my self-worth issues, I began to believe the kids would prefer being with their dad. He could now provide them with the family image that I thought I "should" have. The changes in Jav's relationship provided fertile ground for my self-doubt to flourish. I lived with those beliefs for a year and realized I was miserable. Then I chose to find a way to celebrate both myself and my family. This involved creating a relationship between Ingrid and me. I needed to see us both in a new light.

Ingrid is another avenue of love not just for my children, but for Javier. I did wish him a loving relationship, just as I wish that for myself. If I had chosen ill feelings toward Jav, that is what I would also wish myself. I believe that our feelings toward others often reflect how we feel about ourselves. People who are filled with anger often bring that anger into their relationships as well. People who are peaceful and filled with well being regularly infuse this into their relationships.

Ingrid is also another avenue of love in my life. I would not say that we are best friends. Yet, we do have love for each other and we try to be compassionate and considerate with one another. We also chose not to compete with each other. Competition is always an option between people and we certainly could have been divisive and unfriendly. We are both finding our way and creating a positive relationship.

Ingrid's friends warned her about getting involved with a man who had an ex-wife and children. Everyone around her assumed that this would be an extremely negative situation. Her friends inserted her in the stepmother role between two unhappy divorced people. Interestingly my friends tended to have a negative reaction upon meeting her. The assumption was that we were competing. Friends would rally to help me feel as though I had won the competition. They reacted as though my husband had left me for another woman and, therefore, I needed support. Understandably, everyone acted out of a loving sense to help the one they felt needed support. Curiously, my friends adopted roles of support based on the assumption that Ingrid and I were not amiable. I found it helpful to put forth the idea and the feeling that Ingrid and I were friends/family and that I found her beautiful, loving and a welcome part of my family's life. Simply opening that door helped other people to see the safety in walking through it. It was okay to accept this new member and know that we were creating something that worked for all of us. If we choose love, we can lead others with that same love to a much more positive and loving existence.

Ingrid did not particularly enjoy the label of stepmother, and neither did I. So we found ourselves calling her Ingrid. When my son turned seven, we were having dinner and he said, "I have one mom, one dad and now I have an Ingrid." I was touched by Niky's eloquent verbalization of his understanding of our family. Ingrid came by the next night to bring the children a gift she bought them on a business trip. Ingrid and I stepped outside to say goodbye and I shared what Niky had said the night before. She was very touched by being included in Niky's vision of his family, as they were not married yet. We hugged each other for the first time and I think we, too, had a moment of recognition that we were together.

Susan, a woman in class shared the story of her friendship with her husband's former wife. Susan created a friendship with this woman as she step-parented their two sons. She has since divorced her husband, but continues to have a friendship with this woman as they have a lot in common, both being single parents now. Susan sees this woman as a source of support in her life and feels she offers the same in return. Susan has made a choice about whom she is and the decisions she makes are based on her vision.

I once was speaking to my sister's friend, Dooley, and he referred to families like mine as "broken homes". I reacted strongly to this statement, and I needed to realize why. I interpreted his statement as a negative label that could never be uplifted. Dooley grew up in a family where divorce was not an option. When he did meet others who came from divorced parents, they were, often, troubled and/or economically challenged. I believe this negatively influenced his belief system regarding divorced families. Dooley's comments elicited from me a defensive response. I feared that my family would not be accepted or valued, but viewed as "broken." We all want to be loved, valued and to belong. Therefore, I reacted to Dooley's view of divorced families, because his view mirrored a long-standing fear I had about my own family. I then had to look anew at who I was within my family and how my family lived and thrived as a whole. I saw my family as more communicative, healthy and loving than when we were married. Our family was better than before. We still have problems that arise, but we also have confidence that we can handle everything. I do not see my family as "broken," I see it as being fixed in many ways. I am now always aware of my love feelings for Jav, before my love was buried under anger hurt and resentment. Jav and I love our children, and we continue to build a base support to help them and be their guides in life. Now we have Ingrid's help! We can transcend negative labels. We can re-create in any form we want. It all comes down to the belief in possibilities.

Three years ago I became aware of a parenting class that I thought would benefit my family. I had a friend Andrea, who taught a class called Redirecting Children's Behavior. I invited Ingrid and Jav to join me. Their reaction was interesting. Ingrid immediately said yes while Jav said no. I was reminded of the old joke of women asking for directions and men just wanting to find their own way. After discussing the class with Ingrid, Jav decided to join us. We went every Thursday night to class after having a family dinner at my house. We told our children that we were going to school to learn how to be better parents. Jav, Ingrid and I learned not only about parenting, but also about each other. Participating helped to form a stronger bond between us all. The experience helped to close the seams between our two households affording both the children and ourselves more consistency.

I learned that my parenting style was greatly affected by Jav's parenting style. In other words, if he were authoritarian, I chose to be passive with the children. If he were passive I adopted an authoritarian style. This was a huge revelation to me in that it indicated I was not acting from a centered place, but in reaction to Jav (once again). When I recognized this, it was really time to let go and just be myself. The classes gave us new ideas to develop family time together. Jav and I realized that the children benefited from family time when all of us were together. They seemed calmer and better able to say goodbye to one of us if we spent some quality time together as a family first. We had created something healthy, and we all enjoyed being together.

You cannot do this only for the kids, because it will not work for them if it does not work for you. You cannot fake a relationship for someone else's sake. This is especially true of children, because they are so intuitive and they recognize genuine feelings. Trying to convince children of something that is not there would be an exercise in dishonesty. I am not implying that life is perfect and always happy. We are humans with human emotions and individual reactions to everyone around us. We need effective tools with which to deal with complex interactions within families. Our family finally got to the point of doing family feasts, where everyone in the family gets an individual turn to sit in the middle of a circle. Then we go around and each person tells the person in the middle something they love about that person. This is a wonderful family activity! It was so powerful for Jav and I to say what we loved about each other equally moving was the expressions of love that Ingrid and I shared. I cried, because I was so moved by the beauty of love. I was elated when I noticed my children's smiles as they saw their mother, father and Ingrid share love in an open, honest way.

Creating family time for fun and for closeness is such a fulfilling experience to give ourselves as well as our children. Healthy family time promotes well being. When we love ourselves we can truly love those around us. The willingness to release the bad feelings toward our past marriage partners is crucial. The feelings we have toward others often mirrors our feelings about ourselves. No one benefits from anger and hurt. Everyone gains from love. Which do you choose?

There were new affirmations I adopted in this process of healing. The first declaration I embraced (with life altering consequences was): *There is enough love.* There is enough love in the universe to go around to every human being. When we fill our hearts with love, we tap into the unending supply like the water in the ocean. When we open up to love more will come into our lives. The more you send out to others, the more is returned. Embracing this belief helped me to invite Ingrid into my life and the lives of my children. This affirmation helped me not choose competition and fear as a way of dealing with her, but to embrace the love she brings to my family. I had a choice.

I understood this poignantly one Christmas when I came to pick up my children at Jav and Ingrid's house. Niky and Brontë were showing me all the goodies they had received and I looked over to see my (then four-year-old) daughter, snuggle into Ingrid for a hug. My daughter pressed her cheek into Ingrid's chest and was enfolded in her arms. I recognized the look on my daughter's face as peaceful and loving. I remembered being that age and how it felt to be embraced in loving arms. Brontë looked at me as though to question if what she was doing was acceptable. I looked at her with all the love I felt at that moment. My daughter was being held gently and lovingly. She smiled back and continued her moment with Ingrid. I knew then the moment was about love, and I knew I had a choice about accepting it or rejecting it. I could choose jealousy or I could choose celebration and the latter felt so much better for all concerned. The affirmation that there is enough love helped me to deal with old fears that my children would have more fun with their dad because I felt I offered them less than he did. Once again, I was demeaning my worth and all I do have to offer my children in their life experience. There is enough love for all of us.

One woman in my workshop shared her story of enough love. She was married to her husband who had an affair during their marriage. Their marriage ended but they continued to raise three children together. She gave herself time to heal from the pain of her marriage. A few years later, her parenting partner had a baby with the woman with whom he had an affair. She decided to invite this baby into her family. There was enough love to introduce him as her son's brother and to celebrate this child into her family. The child is included in holidays and weekends. She has given the example of enough love to her three sons as well. They are encouraged to love this new brother. She could have chosen anger and resentment towards this child, and yet she did not.

The second affirmation I adopted was: *There is enough time.* Affirming there is enough time helped me when Jav and I changed our visitation schedule. I was always in a state of unrest because I was constantly reiterating there was not enough time. Believing this caused stress because I always felt the pressure of not accomplishing my responsibilities. Now I tell myself there is enough time and it helps me to be calm and to stay in the moment. If I am in the moment I also have more enjoyment rather than worrying about when it will end or what I must do next. The moment we start thinking about something in the future or a possible problem we have just stepped out of now. Children are masters at staying in the moment. They constantly show us how to be here now. They have not learned the concept of time so one moment stretches on forever because they have no anticipation of what comes next. They live each moment fully. We can do the same.

My third and most challenging affirmation was: *There is enough money.* Divorce creates enormous changes for everyone concerned yet I hate to sum it all up in monetary terms. I never wanted to sit in a courtroom with Jav fighting over money. I felt in my heart that it would demean all that we had created together. One can never put a price tag on life experience. Our culture strongly emphasizes the importance of money, thus it takes precedence over people's emotional well being. I do not mean to belittle anyone's experience in settling financial issues. But I hope to encourage reevaluating the importance of money in the process of divorce.

I waived alimony and agreed with Jav to split the proceeds from the sale of our home. We could have gone on endlessly with attorneys to settle just on that point, and yet that would have cost a fortune both emotionally and financially. Through mediation, Jav set his child support at $500 a month as a sum he could afford. This was a tumultuous and scary time for both of us. I lived for a year with my sister and brother-in-law, because I needed the extra support in every way while Jav and I settled our agreement.

Living with my sister and brother-in-law was difficult for all of us for different reasons. Jav faced the most challenging time because he and my brother-in-law did not get along during this time. Jav's visitation with the children was uncomfortable for everyone and I realized I needed to effect a change. I asked Jav for increased financial support to rent a house on my own with the children. He agreed to double his support so we could start raising our children in a calmer environment. I tried to give Jav the knowledge that everything he helps provide enhances the children's lives. He could write a check each month with resentment in his heart or he could write it with love knowing he is doing the best he can for his children. This might seem inconsequential, however it is powerful. I shared with him that I have faith in him. He must be responsible and truthful about his financial situation. I trust that he does his best because if I sit in question and let doubt arise in me I am the one consumed by all the fear that doubt creates. Jav is the only one who goes to bed knowing in his heart if he is doing the best that he can for his children and I must be willing to let that be his responsibility. My responsibility, every day of my life, is to do my best. We create our own experiences with our children and each other. I am not saying that I would be totally unaffected if Jav chose to not participate financially. However I do have a choice, I can remain angry or I can use the anger as a catalyst for change and find a solution. I would be the one to go to bed with all of that anger and not Jav. Why would I want to do that to myself anymore? So I have given Jav my faith that he is doing all he can for our children. We split the extra-curricular costs and we both volunteer in sports and I volunteer in their classrooms.

Love and trust play key roles in creating relationships just as they do in a marriage. Funny enough, we will always have a relationship with our parenting partners, and we have to decide what we would like that to be. The affirmation there is enough money is helpful because it helps me to know that everyone is doing their best even when it might seem like the opposite. If we see ourselves as victims or being cheated we often feel angry and our children feel that anger. Our bodies and minds pay the high price for keeping all of that anger burning. As Louise Hay points out in her book You Can Heal Your Life, feelings are the result of thoughts and a thought can be changed. Becoming conscious of our thoughts is key. Ernest Holmes, the founder of the Science of Mind philosophy underscored this when he wrote, "Change your thinking, change your life." We can see ourselves anyway we want. How do you see yourself and your situation?

NEW LABEL AND NEW PARTNERS EXERCISE

1. Which old labels do not feel good to you?

_____

_____

_____

_____

2. Which labels or phrases feel positive and celebratory to your family?

_____

_____

_____

_____

3. Are old ways of thought holding you back? Re: money, time, or love, self-esteem?

_____

_____

_____

_____

4. In what ways can you change old thought patterns into helpful fulfilling ideas and ways of thinking?

_____

_____

_____

_____

5. How are new members coming into the family affecting you?

_____

_____

_____

_____

_____

_____

6. How can you make the addition of new members to your family a positive experience?

_____

_____

_____

_____

_____

_____

_____

_____

_____

_____

_____

_____

_____

CHAPTER 11

REDISCOVERING YOURSELF

Start the work in this chapter by asking yourself what makes you happy. What gives you joy? How do you rejuvenate yourself? Write down whatever thoughts come to mind and put them aside for completing the next exercise.

This practice emphasizes getting in touch with ourselves, and understanding who we are. It is important to take care of ourselves just as we do those around us. Think about the following: Is it hard to give to yourself? Do you put it off or feel a need to justify it to yourself and others? Or does the concept of caring for yourself not occur to you at all? Do not feel bad if your answer is yes. The goal is to become aware of your choices and the way you create. If your initial choice does not work for you, then you can always choose differently. We can re-create every day, every five minutes-- *whenever* we want! Even a new thought can change the feel of your day. If you are feeling in a funk, check in with your mental chatter and examine its tone. What thoughts or mantras are you playing back over and over? Just become aware and note what it is. Now try creating a new positive thought on the same subject or just about you and feed that in. You can change your whole being just with your thoughts. Choose consciously your thoughts. They are powerful because they create our moments and our reality. What would you like yours to feel and be like?

I find that the actual practice of self-care is one of the most challenging to master. I speak of this to all my clients, underscoring its importance to their well being. Yet even in my own life, when things begin to get overwhelming, (too many demands at work, my children's schedules increased) the first place I cut out time is usually in the area of my self-care. As individuals, it is obvious we must take care of ourselves, because who else will? As parents, it becomes easy to site the needs of our children as more important. Yet who will be there to care of our children if we are not well? When I question my clients about their week and time appointed to themselves, usually the first thing we all notice is the lack of time actually spent on their well being.

Work and children tend to take the lion's share of time and then we face exhaustion (physically, emotionally and spiritually) because we are running on empty. I recommended to a class that they all get a large board and make a schedule for the week. Each day they had to dedicate time to themselves. When it was in print the women seemed to adhere to this practice much more than when left to the last minute planning.

It is clear that underlying even the loyal dedication of time to ourselves, is the level of self-love we feel. Too often, we feel guilty taking time for ourselves. There is always a worthier cause for our time investment. When will we see our own worth and answer with the words *of course,* I took a nap or a yoga class! The answer is simple, when we <u>choose</u> to do so, and not before. This crucial element, as are most things in our lives, a matter of choice.

Once we truly see ourselves in all of our splendor then the old view tends to crumble and fall away like an old outer shell; leaving a new, bright being underneath just waiting to come out and dance in the light. All we have to do is let it happen.

I have a friend Grace who was married for a number of years and then separated from her husband. They have decided to date one another and are truly enjoying this part of their life together. Grace's friends are admonishing her to let her husband go in order for someone else to come into her life, fearing she will be alone. Grace's response was beautiful and eloquent. She said, "I am not afraid to be alone, in fact, it feels good to have time for myself and still enjoy the company of this man in my life. I can just live in the present moment, and I don't need to make an immediate decision."

I see Grace as a role model for others---showing we need not be afraid to be without someone in our lives. Having a partner does not indicate our worth. All is well for Grace and she is learning a lot about herself by being with herself quietly. People often succumb to the fear of being alone and choose a partner who is unsuitable simply to fill a void. There are a lot of distractions in our culture, so many that we need not spend a moment on introspection if we choose. There is television, social events, sports and the great American past time of shopping to keep us all occupied instead of focusing our attention upon ourselves. I had to go within and spend time alone to meet my inner self. This was not easy nor was I without fear doing this. The quiet was essential for me, but it was not a widely popular choice.

I turned off my television three years ago and it has been a very positive experience. A few things were evident immediately, I interacted more with my children and they used their imagination more in their play time. Over time, I realized I became less physically fearful. I no longer watched violent images or emotional dramas (that were not mine) before going to bed. I realized most of the programming for children was either violent as well or completely without any beauty or poetry. I no longer feared being alone in my own home at night. I no longer had an unattainable example, blinking at me constantly, of what I should look like, dress like, or act like, in order to be accepted in society. Therefore, I seemed much more ready and able to accept myself as I was. I am behind in news, and the latest eye catching commercials --- but I am also quite happy. I spend my evenings reading and writing. My children and I snuggle up after homework and dinner to read together before bed. It is quiet and peaceful and I love it!

The patterns that we continue to repeat in our lives exemplify the level of belief in ourselves and our self-love. Everything can be reduced finally to this one thing. Speaking with clients, friends and family, I see that each of us has a particular set of beliefs about who we are and our worth from our family of origin. We seem to spend most of our adult lives trying to overcome and eventually change the image we have of self. I recently became interested in the work of Dr. Michael Newton, when I read his book, *Journey of Souls*. Newton recorded his patients' experiences under hypnosis and detailed the process of souls choosing their next life. Our lives are about self-discovery. He presents evidence, based on his research that says, we choose a life here with a broad possibility of experiencing exactly that which we would like for our own individual evolution as a soul. We all experience a form of amnesia in order to be fully engaged in the life we have chosen. Free will is, however, the purpose of reincarnation.

All of this continues to suggest a recurring pattern of forgetting, experiencing and remembering in life for all of us. I think it is interesting to underscore the existence of free will. We all have choices about how we create our lives. I have met many people who seem to readily understand the meaning of life; have remembered who they are and are beacons of light. Still others seem lost in a thick fog, unable to see beyond their own front door. I have come to believe that there is never a life wasted. Some souls might not have full enlightenment upon their life's meaning during their time on this plane. It might not occur until they leave earth, but I believe full understanding comes to each soul about his/her life experience and choices.

As Paul Ferrini, states in his book, *Love Without Conditions,* our self view is largely effected by our family of origin because we are all conditioned to value ourselves only when people respond to us positively. He states that beginning to give love to the wounded part of us inside begins to reverse our belief of our self worth being determined by others around us. We must learn how to value ourselves as we are here and now and without conditions. We demonstrate love by giving it unconditionally to ourselves, as we do this we then attract others into our lives who can love us without conditions. Ferrini states that when we know we are worthy of love we often interpret the actions of others in a loving way. We are not hurt easily. Instead of feeling victimized by a rude person we tend to see the other person as having a challenge in *their* day. Our view of our lives is greatly affected by how worthy or loveable we feel we are.

Neale Donald Walsch, the author of *Conversations With God* books introduced me to the idea of creating the grandest version of the greatest vision I ever held of myself. Walsch helped me put into perspective all that I am and all that I want to create. This writing is part of my grandest vision because it is all about love. This book acknowledges the importance of love and our ability to give and receive it. When I feel myself slipping, I have to remind

100

myself that there is love in me and all around me. All I have to do is accept it.

When my six-year old daughter, Brontë, was acting out after school, I found myself frustrated with her behavior. When we were calm and quiet, she told me that she did not feel loved because we did not have enough time together anymore. She said that I did not rock her in my lap like I used to do. She had just come back from her dad's the night before and a special sleep over at her cousin's the night before that. She was saying that she needed to feel close and connected right now. I noticed how clearly she asked for the love she wanted. When she asked, I could understand and take her in my lap. How often do we communicate this clearly in asking for the love we want? We can ask just like this six-year old did and know, like she, that we deserve this love, and it is there to receive. It is also there to give.

There is a huge shift that happens after divorce in that you have to find your balance again. You are balancing on your own which is a different feeling after being married. You might notice you have more time to dedicate to yourself. What are your needs and what things work best for you? You may find you have changed tremendously from the person you were when you married. We often give up certain parts of ourselves or tone them way down in order to keep someone else in the relationship. Sometimes this happens to keep ourselves in the relationship. Now is the time to give ourselves the freedom to expand.

The most important part of rediscovering ourselves, is believing we are whole and complete. Another part of this process is taking care of ourselves with healthful, wonderful things such as; quiet time, good food, exercise, time with friends and time to laugh. I thought it was interesting to see that even in my parenting class the first topic was care of the self. The curriculum devotes two pages to ideas on how to care for the self. We must be well in order to take care of our children. Taking care of ourselves provides a wonderful role model for our children to emulate in their lives. I often tell my children when I leave for my yoga class that it keeps me healthy in my body and my heart so that I can be a caring mom to them. At first, they saw yoga as just time away from them. After a time they became accustomed to my schedule, and my daughter started to imitate my yoga poses!

After divorce, you might find yourself with some free time without your children, due to sharing time with a parenting partner. Reflect thoughtfully about how you would like to spend this time. Utilize this time for yourself in positive ways. What interests do you have? What did you never give yourself the time to explore?

For a time, I filled both of my weekly free nights with yoga classes. I was a dedicated student for two and a half years. Starting a yoga practice taught me so much about myself and about life. Yoga is about being with the self quietly and getting in touch with your higher self. I had a good friend who started a yoga studio in her home, and my sister and I went to learn from her. She not only taught yoga, but cooked a delicious meal for us afterward, which we ate by candlelight on the floor. This was an amazing time in my life. I remember her covering me with a blanket the first time after the practice when you lie down to rest. It made me cry because it had been so long since I had felt nurtured. In reality, it had been so long since *I* nurtured myself.

Yoga gave my body strength and flexibility and it gave my spirit nurturing, strength and recognition. It gave my mind the ability to relax and to be quiet. I now have a practice on my own at home, and I also practice at a studio once a week. I would highly recommend yoga to anyone. When I was in my anger phase I spent two years running at full speed on a treadmill for forty-five minutes just to find release. Then came yoga. I also introduced meditation into my life. This has changed so much in my daily life. I try to start my days with meditation, which helps set the tone.

For many of us, the idea of giving to ourselves might seem foreign or downright wrong. Yet it is essential and it is all about self-love and honoring who we are. If we do not honor ourselves who will? My sister often says that no one will love you better than you love yourself. Look at this statement for a moment. How would you like others to treat you? Would you choose love, respect, honesty, caring, compassion, understanding, gentleness, joy etc? Do you give this to yourself or do you just reserve this for others? Again, no one will love you better than you love yourself. You are stating to the world your worth and what you deserve by how you love yourself.

What would we like to teach our children? Would we like to teach them to love and care for themselves? The best way to teach children is by example. If we are not modeling self-love for our children they will not know this as adults. Adults often refer back to old maps of behavior when faced with new situations. We can start now to forge new territory. We can come back to a place of celebrating who we are, as children do most naturally when they are young. They know who they are and they are happy with that knowledge. We can be, too. We are all deserving, magnificent beings. We are all whole and complete. We can create whatever we would like, life is wide open and full of possibilities. We must declare who we are and what we want.

This chapter seeks to demonstrate the absolute necessity for self-love. All we owe others is to be well ourselves. Imagine what the world would be like if we really knew and acknowledged this in our souls. We all come from the same source. We all live the same lives with a few different characteristics. Look closely and you will see a bit of yourself in everyone else's story. We all want the same things: to be valued, to be loved, and to belong. Sharing this material with others strengthens ones own understanding of this process. We best teach what we need to learn.

A guiding question in dealing with difficult situations is; *What would love do now?* I find that this question always quiets anger, and eases frustration, and helps me to see everyone in a more tender and compassionate light. It helps guide me to be who I am and who I want to be. My friend Hilary gave me a beautiful quote by a master teacher, Nelson Mandela:

> Our deepest fear is not that we are inadequate.
> Our deepest fear is that we are powerful

beyond measure. It is our light, not our darkness that most frightens us. We ask ourselves "Who am I to be brilliant, gorgeous talented and fabulous?" Actually, who are you not to be? You are a child of God. Your playing small does not serve the world. There's nothing enlightened in shrinking so others don't feel insecure around you. We are born to make manifest the glory of God that is within us. It is not just in some of us; it is in everyone and as we let our own light shine, we unconsciously give other people permission to do the same. As we are liberated from our fear, from our own fear, our presence automatically liberates others.

I was so moved by this quote that it stays on my refrigerator along with a poem my son wrote to me and a prayer for healing. These are the thoughts with which we need to fill ourselves on a daily basis.

My mind was a negative time bomb going off at regular intervals before and after my divorce. Each of the following books came into my life at a time when I was ready for their messages and when I most needed them. I thank the authors for their inspirational words, which helped me to re-create my life. I would highly recommend the following books:

Louise Hays, *You Can Heal Your Life*

Daphne Rose Kingma, *The Future Of Love*

Paul Ferrini, *Love Without Conditions*

Neale Donald Walsch, *Conversations With God and Uncommon Dialogues*

Jon Kabat-Zinn, *Wherever You Go There You Are*

Sark, *Succulent Wild Woman*

Sark, *Transformation Soup*

Caroline Myss, *Anatomy Of The Spirit* and *Sacred Contracts*

These books have given me great insight and taught me much over the past three years. They have given me gifts with which to understand my life and what I have created. These books reaffirm my ability to make choices, my belief in myself and my resolve to move forward.

REDISCOVERING YOURSELF EXERCISE

1. List any interests that you never had time to explore and develop.

    _____

    _____

    _____

2. What do you love to do?

    _____

    _____

    _____

    _____

    _____

3. Is it difficult for you to dedicate time to yourself? Does this bring on guilt? What is your immediate response to the idea of time for yourself?

    _____

    _____

    _____

    _____

    _____

    _____

    _____

    _____

    _____

4. What did you learn about yourself from your response to question 3? What is your view on taking care of yourself?

_____

_____

_____

_____

_____

5. What is something you can do to honor yourself? (for example creating a meditation place, developing a spiritual practice etc.)

_____

_____

_____

_____

_____

6. List ten things you love about yourself.

_____

_____

_____

_____

_____

_____

_____

_____

_____

7. Make a plan for the week and devote thirty minutes to one hour to yourself each day. What will you do with your time?

_____

_____

_____

_____

_____

_____

_____

_____

_____

_____

_____

_____

_____

_____

_____

_____

_____

_____

_____

_____

_____

_____

CHAPTER 12

THE PROCESS

I realize after working on re-creating my relationship with Jav for the past six years, that the process of doing so is just as meaningful as the end result. By merely sharing everyday life with my family I continue to learn much about myself. My life is so enriched because of the family and friends with whom I am blessed. The process of getting back to a place of love with Jav has not always been smooth. There have been many times that we took one step forward and two big steps back. Regardless, we continue to re-create. There have been many opportunities to become embroiled in anger and remain there. Ultimately, we pay a very high price for that choice. We are all capable of releasing anger and creating different life experiences. We need only decide who we are and what we want. This is the first step in re-creating.

I have been separated from Jav for six years now, and we have come a long way in that time. Last year, we went on our first vacation together with our children. We went skiing in Idaho for five days. His wife, Ingrid, could not come with us because she had just started a new job and was not yet eligible for vacation time. I invited both Jav and Ingrid to come and share the moment with the kids and me. Ingrid chose to encourage Jav to come with me, because she knew how badly he wanted to take the kids skiing. This was Jav's favorite sport, and he had always imagined skiing with the children. Ingrid was in her heart when she told him to go skiing with his ex-wife and his children. This seemed to be an easy decision for her based on her love for her husband. I know that it could not have been easy for her, feeling like her whole family was off on a vacation while she was at home working. Yet she stood by her decision and dealt with all the emotions that arose during that time.

Surprisingly, this trip afforded tremendous healing. I have not spent an entire day with Jav since we were married and our marriage ended with such negative emotions. Suddenly, Jav and I were able to see one another in a new light and wish each other well. We had the opportunity to play and enjoy our children together. Jav and I had lunch one day in the lodge and we had a conversation about our marriage. We acknowledged that we had done our best in our marriage for whom we were then, and we took steps toward healing old hurts. The hurt was gone—leaving more room for tenderness. There was a lot of emotion and a lot of love, but it was not romantic love. It was the love between two people who have shared a life together and recognize that love still exists. The time we shared was very comforting and soothing. We actually had a conversation about the children he and Ingrid plan to have. I told Jav I thought it would be good to have another baby in the family and that it will be a special moment to hold their baby, because he or she will be my children's brother or sister. I volunteered for baby-sitting now and then on Saturday nights so they can have a night out, and we both laughed through our tears.

Jav and I both had the chance to be playful and relaxed and most of all to be *friends*. We saw each other differently than we did six years prior; our eyes were no longer shaded by hurt and anger. We had a fresh vision and I think we have kept it in many ways. Our children experienced their parents being good to one another and sharing time and fun together. They enjoyed this vacation enormously. I feel as though we gave each other and our children a gift on that trip, because it helped us all move forward. In a way, Ingrid also gave us this gift, because regardless of her participation - she gave her blessing.

My family is and will continue to be a work in progress. We continue to shift, evolve and change like any family-- we just do it in *two* homes. My family is capable of creating whatever it wishes. We still have our trying times, and there are those never-ending cycles that take time and care. Through it all, I am confident that we will work things out and find solutions that will remedy any situation. It is important to have the desire to resolve problems. I have confidence Jav and Ingrid will continue to communicate with me in an effort to work things out together. I know that I must continue to ask for what I need in the relationship, as well.

While Jav, Ingrid and I continue to have our trying moments, I think we now have a grasp of the important points. We understand that this is our family. We respect that we all want to participate in our children's lives. We also respect each other and our desire to be present. The members of our family all have a sense of belonging and of being loved, which helps us overcome challenges common among two home families. We participate as a family in events at school. We plan the children's birthdays together and share the details. We help our children celebrate mother's and father's day with the other parent. We do all of this because it feels good.

I want to emphasize the cyclical nature of our relationships. The relationship between Jav and me is much like a marriage--- effort and intentions are required to facilitate our communication. I walked away from our ski trip feeling as though we had hit new heights in understanding and supporting one another, and that problems were miles away. In a sense, that was exactly true in that moment. Yet one year later, I find my family cycling into a challenging situation. The present problem involves child support. I hesitated to write about this because it seems so revealing, and yet that was exactly my goal. I wanted to share my family's creation with others rebuilding after divorce.

My parenting partner found himself in the position of having to cut his child support payment in half due to his financial circumstances. This meant he would be going back to the amount in our original agreement. He implied he might be unable to fulfill even that commitment. When Jav related this to me, my heart sank to my stomach. I was terrified of being solely financially responsible for our children. I found myself feeling as though I were re-living the scenario of six years ago when we separated. I again experienced the fear of being without money to support my children, and it became evident to me that I had strong feelings attached to that past experience. I also had difficulty understanding Jav and Ingrid's ability to buy a bigger more expensive house while reducing child support. This period led to powerful conversations between all three of us. Due to money, I suddenly became doubtful about all we had created together. I felt as though everything I had worked to create for the past six years was now somehow invalid. Once again, Jav and I were struggling with an old issue.

Ingrid, Jav and I had a powerful exchange, in which I told Jav I felt his actions were irresponsible, when he replied I had ruined his life six years ago. I realized that we were in two different places in our healing. I took his anger personally, as being directed toward me. I finally understood that his anger was toward himself and his present situation. Not feeling guilty about Jav's statement to me, and knowing that we were jointly responsible, was a defining moment for me. He still saw me as solely responsible for ending our marriage. I now understand that we are all responsible for our own healing, and not that of others. I told Jav that he can always remain a man whose life was ruined by me, the woman he married, or he can see all the wonder of his life, two great children and a wife who loved him. The choice was his. I had the same choice. I could see myself constantly financially victimized by my partner, or I could envision myself putting all my energy into creating a framework that enabled me to handle whatever arose.

People tend to negate all that is here now if they remain in the past and attached to anger, hurt and fear. I realized I was still attached to the fear of my monetary situation with Jav. Ultimately, this has allowed me to look again at old fears about our financial relationship and to finally set them free. My fear that Jav would someday not meet his financial responsibilities was realized in my view. I have always believed that we create situations to help us face our worst fears in order to see there is nothing to fear. While my partner's modification of child support did not inspire gratitude, I am thankful for that which I did gain from this experience—the courage to face my financial fears, the inspiration to complete this book, and the confidence to support my family.

I now see how I was isolating myself in this dilemma and, therefore, making everything worse. I had convinced myself that Jav was doing this out of anger toward me and, meanwhile, living an abundant life with his wife. These thoughts led me to step back from Jav and Ingrid and to surround myself in my fear. I finally spoke to Jav and shared my thoughts. He was surprised to hear how I had interpreted his actions. He explained that he was struggling with his new job and not earning much money. He was borrowing funds from his parents to meet his household needs and to satisfy child support obligations. Jav was struggling with his own self-esteem concerning his current income status and had been working hard in the last three years to find work. I realized I had made Jav the villain in my drama when we both seemed to have financial problems. Again, I have the choice of finding solutions or staying angry and afraid. Re-creating the vision of myself and creating this book have been instrumental in guiding me through this challenging cycle of our relationship. I am not a master of this process; rather I am a student diligently applying to my life lessons learned. Reaffirming and practicing the concepts in this book enabled me to move forward.

I have examined and reexamined my emotional reactions to the financial dilemmas that Jav and I have created, trying to glean some information that would be helpful. I have noted my fear and the underlying self worth issues in doubting my capabilities of supporting myself and my children. The self-doubt is at the root of my reactions to this drama. I re-acted in the same old way I did before to this situation. When Jav would face financial challenges and I would then feel the repercussions, I felt left adrift and took everything personally between us. Then fear and hurt became my constant companions once again. I now realize the work I must do to gain trust in myself. I must trust on a higher level that all is well and will continue to be. I am more than capable and my children and I will be provided for in our lives. I must constantly remind myself not to take my partner's actions personally.

Having this trust and faith also frees Jav and I to continue to create a relationship that works for both of us. We are just a man and a woman, a mom and a dad raising our children and finding our way back. There is still work to do. The work and the need for it is clear. Considering all the work I have already done, I now see the possible results before the work is complete. The possibilities for the outcome beckon me, encourage me and set me on my path.

My vision is set and my direction is known. I am confident I will learn a tremendous amount on the way. I will gain insights. Both me and my family will receive the gifts from this journey together.

Ingrid, Jav and I are working hard to come to a mutual understanding, regarding financial support and shared responsibility. This can be challenging when people have different views. I believe that we are a team and that we will support ourselves, one another and our children accordingly. The best we can do is to continue to communicate, and search for answers that support all of us.

I share this part of my life to underline the importance of the process of re-creating a love relationship after divorce. Regardless of what we have created together, we are constantly changing and evolving. Therefore, we will always have new conditions within which to experience ourselves. We have choices about our thoughts and about our actions and, ultimately, who we want to be.

The way in which I have re-created my life after divorcing my husband is one way, but it is not the only way. I have written about my family's personal struggles and triumphs, as well as my own in order to demonstrate that we are not alone. However, we are capable of change, choice and creating whatever we would like to experience. Through forgiveness and seeing our partners through fresh eyes we can begin to let go of the negative emotions which restrict our ability to be present in our lives. By taking responsibility for our part in the relationship with our partners, we can better understand who we are and what we would like to change in order to create differently in the future. We must ask for the support we need to help us move forward. Honesty with our children is key to helping them deal with our family situations, as well as beginning the healing process. Our vision is possible, but it does require dedication and commitment to become reality. Embracing the practice of self-love is at the core of this work. The choice, as always, is our own.

I have had a lot of support in the past five years from my mother who never faltered in her love and support of my choices. I have two uncles who decided to become constant supports in my family's life. I am blessed with a sister who is my soul mate and a constant help in reminding me who I am and who I want to be in life. I have Jav, who shared an eight-year marriage, who continues to share two incredible children with me, and remains my friend. I also have Ingrid who mirrors back who I am and loves my children. Above all, I have two great children who share my life, Brontë and Niky. They are truly my teachers in life who remind me of all the important things: forgiveness, playing, laughing, touching and loving. I am truly blessed.

RESOURCES:

Inner Quest
Patty Kishiyama   Certified Clinical Hypnotherapist
1049 Camino Del Mar #7 Del Mar, CA 92014
858 793-7909

Yoga By Jyl
Jyl Auxter
Private and class instruction
914 Highland Ave. Del Mar, CA 92014
858 794-9529
www.yogabyjyl.com

Peaceful Parenting
Andrea Berl
Licensed instructor for the Network for Children and Families
858 259-8898
aberl@san.rr.com

Susan Dale, LCSW
Psychotherapist, Art Therapy
Specializing in Divorce Issues (adults & children)
136 North Acacia ste.A
Solana Bch., CA 92075
858 259-1336

Quantum Energetics
Silja Bjorklund
760 942-0057

Innerlight
Dr. Rick Jelisich
Life Readings, Flower Readings, Healer Training
760 420-8100

Accupuncture and Chinese Herbologist
Sherri Laine
858 259-7444

Astrologist
Natal and/or Progressed Charts
Jo Barginear
281 496-7008

Neale Donald Walsch
Author/Speaker
www.CWG.org

The Collaborative Family Law Group of San Diego
A cooperative approach to separation, divorce and custody
disputes
888 837-9700

Co-Mamas LLC
www.comamas.com
760 942-4572

ShareKids
This tool facilitates planning for the welfare of the children. It
minimizes stressful discussions and possible confrontations
between parents who are divorced or separated.
www.sharekids.com

Printed in the United States
44888LVS00002B/58-60